CW01425019

Seen and Not Heard

Voices of Young British Muslims

Sughra Ahmed

Policy Research Centre

Copyright © Policy Research Centre 2009

All rights reserved. No part of this publication may be reproduced, stored in a retrieval system, or transmitted in any form or by any means, electronic, mechanical, photocopying, recording or otherwise, without the prior permission of the copyright owner.

Copy editing: Julie Pickard
Typsetting: Chat Noir Design
Printing: Ashford Colour Press

ISBN: 978-0-9561418-0-4

Published by

Policy Research Centre
Islamic Foundation, Ratby Lane, Markfield, Leicestershire LE67 9SY, UK

Tel: 01530 244944, Fax: 01530 244946
E-mail: info@policyresearch.org.uk
Web: www.policyresearch.org.uk

Contents

About the Policy Research Centre

The Policy Research Centre, based at the Islamic Foundation, specialises in research, policy advice and training on issues related to British Muslims. The Centre brings together policy, academic and community expertise to inform and shape current policy thinking. We work with civil society, Muslim communities and government, serving as a hub of analysis and communication on policy matters and to foster good community relations.

The Centre seeks to:

○ Enhance the policy responses to some of the critical issues being debated today around identity, citizenship and security.

○ Raise awareness of social policy concerns impacting on the lives of Muslim citizens.

○ Inform communities about policy debates and the policy-making process.

Acknowledgements

The author would like to thank members of the Policy Research Centre for their help and constant support, especially Naved Siddiqi and Samina Ali both of whom were involved in the research. The generous donations from the Edith Murphy Foundation and the UK Islamic Mission made this report possible as well as insights and advice from Rachel Briggs, Hannah Lownsbrough, Tafazal Mohammad, Alveena Malik and Anam Hoque, all of whom offered unique perspectives on young Muslims through theory and practice.

Insights and advice from Rachel Briggs, Hannah Lownsbrough, Tafazal Mohammad, Alveena Malik and Anam Hoque, provided the research with unique perspectives on young Muslims through theory and practice.

Finally, and most importantly, gratitude goes to the research participants who gave their time willingly for interviews, focus groups and a roundtable discussion at various stages of the research. Without the genuine thoughts and comments from young people this research would not have been possible – thank you!

Foreword by the Bishop of Leicester

Successive generations face issues of identity and citizenship. The question of who we are, as a nation and as individuals, is very pertinent at this present time, especially among young people who live in a fast-moving and technologically advanced world. They attract a good deal of media attention, much of it critical, offered often without an in-depth analysis of their needs and lifestyle expectations.

We need as a society to understand one another across cultural and faith boundaries. In our diverse communities up and down the country young people live, study and work alongside one another, without at times fully understanding each other. Within each of our own cultural and faith communities we are also guilty of not understanding our young people. As a Christian leader I am committed to allowing young people to find their voice within the Church, and throughout society, so that their views can be heard and their contribution to society recognised and affirmed.

We currently are repeatedly given invitations to question the contribution of Muslims in our society. Muslim youth are like any other group of young people – they want to be heard and affirmed by all sections of our society that includes, supports and resources them. I am glad that this report shows the true face of Muslim young people as eager to engage in our society and wanting to be taken seriously for their contribution.

As this report suggests, "much is written about young Muslims but we rarely seem to actually hear their voices". This report goes a long way to rectifying this issue so that young Muslim voices are heard and valued within Islam and throughout wider society.

I commend it to you.

The Right Reverend Tim Stevens
The Lord Bishop of Leicester
Chair of the Trustees of The Children's Society

1

Executive Summary

The key aim of this research project is to identify the areas of concern that young Muslims feel are pertinent to their lives. Within this framework, the project sought to:

○ Explore the scope of intergenerational experiences specific to young Muslims and probe into their effects

○ Explore to a reasonable degree the level and type of influence a contact with Islamic teachings has on young Muslim men and women; and explore the extent of and the tensions of this on the lives of young people

○ Explore the impact of the media on the self-perception of young Muslims; and probe the extent of this impact in the areas of social exclusion, identity and self-esteem

○ Provide a feedback mechanism to reflect these issues back to policy makers and community leaders.

The Policy Research Centre conducted this research in order to gain an increased awareness of young Muslims' thinking and opinions on a range of topics. By way of comparison the report briefly looks into the context of youth work conducted by the Church of England and the State.

Throughout this research various qualitative investigations were made, including nine focus groups (talking to over 100 young people) across the UK, nine interviews with experts, as well as desk research and attendance of youth events.

This is the first study of its kind exploring issues simultaneously across a spectrum of British cities with young Muslims. The study enabled the researcher to gain an insight across many different experiences and helped in creating discussions around the following themes:

○   Identity, belonging and citizenship

○   Mainstream and religious issues around engagement and integration as well as leadership and role models

○   Media and its impact on a young Muslim's life

○   Intergenerational experiences.

Recommendations

The recommendations presented below have been derived directly from conversations with young people during the course of the research. An implementation of these and further research would serve to address some of the key issues which young Muslims are grappling with daily.

Investing in the future

1.   A national Muslim heritage programme to be funded which looks at capturing the experiences of Muslim pioneers arriving post World War II and integrating into British life. The project would highlight lessons learnt from such experiences which can inform a sense of 'Britishness' for younger Muslims, as well as instilling a sense of local pride and identity, and inspiring greater stakeholdership.

2.   Government funding to allow groups providing faith and culturally sensitive counselling and support to extend such work outside London. Every major city in the UK should have support services such as those provided by the Muslim Youth Helpline.

3. Government funding to support youth activities through new small grants programmes over multiple years to achieve longevity.

4. Increased investment by trusts, foundations and bodies such as the National Council for Voluntary Youth Services (NCVYS) into work among young Muslims. This will help organisations to become less reliant on government grants and allows for a greater development of civil society.

Local service providers

1. Joined-up services at the local level (similar to the Integrated Youth Services Hub in Leicester) among agencies whose work impacts on young Muslims and the inclusion of youth and community representatives on these teams.

2. Local service providers need to find ways to work directly with a wider range of young people, for example the 'Youth Offer',[1] which aims to reflect the needs of all young people through their participation at a local level.

3. Regeneration projects in areas with strong concentrations of Muslims should take particular account of the needs that may be specific to young Muslims, especially at the planning phase of service delivery. Enhancements in consultation, information provision and assessment processes will enable service providers to identify how services can better match their service provision to meet the needs of young Muslims which may be currently overlooked.

4. Targeted and high-quality support for professionals working with young Muslims to understand specific religious and cultural challenges facing them and the barriers to accessing state youth services.

5. More focused, assertive mentoring and work-based learning schemes offering development plans. These should use quick and direct feedback mechanisms and present the opportunity to increase skills as well as offer information, advice, guidance and possible routes to employment and/or educational opportunities.

---

1 A national initiative which aims to tackle poor youth services across England and include teenagers in consultations around local youth service provision.

Education and schools

1. Use the new duty on schools to promote community cohesion to enable better integration of Muslims into British society through:

   a. Muslim heritage and contribution to civilisation past and present encompassed into aspects of teaching, learning and curricula.

   b. Direct academic intervention programmes being focused on Muslim boys to achieve the equity and excellence strand of the new duty.

   c. Schools becoming 'safe and neutral places' for local communities to come together and interact with one another. School outreach programmes could look at how to directly meet the learning needs of Muslim parents and wider communities that are currently inhibited from full participation in civil and political life.

2. Long-term school-linking exchange programmes between schools with young people from different ethnic profiles embedded within school ethos with the purpose of ensuring that more meaningful relationships are formed.

3. Schools should create opportunities for elderly Muslims to speak to younger Muslims. Examples of work amongst Gypsy and Traveller communities as well as white working-class groups in some London boroughs shows that such intergenerational encounters work well. Often the best projects are two-way processes where young people teach older generations new skills and older people teach young people life skills.

Muslim voluntary sector and mosques

1. Mosques should have dedicated outreach programmes services and facilities to meet the needs of young people.

2. Management committees in mosques should ensure that imams and community leaders who engage with youth have adequate training in meeting the needs of young people.

3. Voluntary sector organisations can reach a sizeable number of young Muslims; such organisations would benefit from specialised youth skills training.

4. Through mentoring and educational support programmes (such as projects initiated by Mosaic and the City Circle), Muslim professionals could significantly invest in the development of young people.

5. Increasingly madrasahs are teaching more than rote learning. This needs more concerted attention and madrasahs need to teach the understanding of the text as well as relating it to the lived reality of young British Muslims.

Media

1. There is a need for more events such as workshops that can enhance media literacy among young people and give increased contact with journalists and programme makers, as well as provide an opportunity to air concerns and anxieties, to create two-way conversations.

2. Employers in the media should increase awareness of recruitment opportunities and career pathways in the industry, specifically targeting young Muslims.

Policing

1. The police should create more avenues for young people to better understand police services, shadow officers and interact in ways that can develop learning in both directions.

2. The police should work with non-police partners to inform young people of their rights and responsibilities as well as complaints procedures regarding policing. This is particularly important when young Muslims are feeling targeted by measures such as 'stop and search'.

3. The Independent Police Complaints Commission (IPCC) should develop partnerships with suitable Muslim organisations to collate data on complaints about police procedures from Muslim citizens (given that some young Muslims may be reluctant to approach the IPCC directly).

Further research

1. Increased funding for targeted, thematic research into the specific areas highlighted in this report.

2. A revisit of the Cantle Report (2001) and an assessment of the progress on matters relating to cohesion and young people, eight years on, especially in light of the 2007 duty on schools to promote cohesion.

3. There is a need to examine the use of terminology such as cohesion, Preventing Violent Extremism (PVE) and integration. For many these terms have become synonymous with the use of social vehicles to achieve political outcomes. As a result many local communities resist (even resent) the terms and therefore may not engage in the discourse.

2

Introduction

They ask us to integrate, then they come and ask you who you are and class me as Pakistani; if you can't see me as British how can you understand me?

Much is written about young Muslims but we rarely seem to actually hear their voices. This report is an attempt to bring the voices of young British Muslims to the fore, to enable their thoughts and opinions to be heard by those who seek to engage them. By enabling such voices we hear how young British Muslims feel about how they are perceived by others, and their desire to be understood as British Muslims. This research set out to talk to young British Muslims about topical issues while listening to their recommendations on possible solutions to long-running policy dilemmas and barriers to meaningful engagement. We found focus group participants to be communicative of current challenges while proposing opportunities to resolve some of the current issues in relation to the media, education and intergenerational experiences, among others.

Young British Muslims are an important component of British society and policy makers ought to be aware of the potential contribution this growing generation of young British Muslims stands to make in the future of British life.

The key aim of this research project was to identify the areas of concern that young Muslims themselves feel are pertinent to their lives. Within this framework, the project sought to:

○ Explore the scope of intergenerational experiences specific to young Muslims and probe into their effects

○ Explore to a reasonable degree the level and type of influence a contact with Islamic teachings has on young Muslim men and women; and explore the extent of and the tensions of this on the lives of young people

○ Explore the impact of the media on the self-perception of many young Muslims; and probe the extent of this impact in the areas of social exclusion, identity and self-esteem

○ Provide a feedback mechanism to reflect these issues back to policy makers and community leaders.

The Policy Research Centre conducted this research in order to gain an increased awareness of young Muslims' thinking and opinions on a range of topics. By way of comparison the report briefly looks into the context of youth work conducted by the Church of England and the State. Do the challenges differ from one community to the next? What resources are being invested into youth work? The recommendations this research seeks to make begin answering the questions for three key stakeholder groups: policy makers, statutory services and Muslim communities.

The word 'youth' has different meanings depending on the context. According to the *World Youth Report 2003* the term youth, or young people, is used as a statistical artefact to refer specifically to those aged 15–25 years (Youth at the United Nations, 2003). This is done for ease of comparison, as it is the age grouping for which data are available. However, the designation is often too narrow when young people and their circumstances are considered on a country by country basis. Another definition, used in discussion of the policy responses of governments to particular problems faced by young people, is based on a sociological definition of youth as a transition stage between childhood and adulthood. More precisely, it comprises a series of transitions "from adolescence to adulthood, from dependence to independence, and from being recipients of society's services to becoming contributors to national economic, political, and cultural life" (Youth at the United Nations, 2003, p. 74). This definition will be explored later in chapter 4, 'Literature Review: Young, British and Muslim', in light of youth culture.

This research project is designed to identify some of the pertinent issues relating to young Muslims. We highlight some of these concerns, and go into detail as to the reason why young people themselves feel such issues exist and explore the impact of these areas on young people, as well as wider society.

We began the project with the hypothesis that issues of concern would include education (religious and non-religious), identity, belonging and citizenship, the media, community leadership as well as discrimination, delinquency and policing. This hypothesis was tested to clarify the precise factors that impact on young Muslims who participated in this research process.

To understand the challenges young Muslims are grappling with is key to understanding British Muslim communities in their entirety. Official statistics (which are a mixture of data based on ethnicity and religion) show that over 50% of Muslims in Britain are under the age of 25, and 35% of Pakistanis and 38% of Bangladeshi and other Black and minority ethnic (BME) groups are thought to be under the age of 16 (ONS, 2001).

Recent figures show the following:

○ In 2001 there were nearly 1.6 million Muslims in Great Britain (ONS, 2001)

○ The largest ethnic groups among British Muslims are: Pakistani (over 42%), Bangladeshi (over 16%) and Indian (over 8%) (ONS, 2001)

○ The average age of a Muslim is 28 years old, 13 years below the national average and nearly half (46%) of all British Muslims were born in the UK (Khan, 2008)

○ Bangladeshi and Pakistani pupils performed below the national average across all Key Stages in 2007 (DCSF, 2007)

○ Approximately 3% of Muslim pupils attend Muslim faith schools (Association of Muslim Schools, 2007)

○ Rates of child poverty are especially high for Pakistani (60%) and Bangladeshi (72%) children compared with white children (25%) (DWP, 2006).

The proportion of young Muslims is higher than the average of any other religious community in the country and warrants a significant level of research to better our understanding of British Muslims. What can they contribute as citizens? And how can policy makers, statutory services and the Muslim communities enable this contribution more effectively? These three sectors are key in the growth of young people as they directly impact on their lives and the society in which they live. It is important for these constituencies to gain a better understanding and become familiar with the issues Muslim youth themselves feel are pertinent to them.

Government (central, regional and local) has the responsibility of creating policy frameworks and legislating on areas that affect Muslim youth directly; some of these are well being, life chances, community services, poverty, education, housing, employment and counter-terrorism legislation such as Section 44 of the Terrorism Act 2000.

The success of policies aimed at controlling behaviour is partly dependent on trust. Government initiatives aimed at Muslim youth, to a degree, rely on research to gain an informed understanding of how young people perceive these policies and why. But where does trust lie? What factors influence trust and can they be determined, either through a synthesis of research efforts to date or through further study? And how easy is it to win this trust?

A recent government initiative has brought together a group of young Muslims from across England to form the Young Muslims Advisory Group (YMAG), which was described by government as "the next generation of Muslim community leaders". YMAG is a formal attempt at harnessing the opinions of Muslim youth in order to help educate and direct government thinking on areas such as education, employment and "reducing teenage pregnancy and tackling use of drugs and alcohol by young people" (DCLG, 2008). Although the remit of the YMAG is broader than the stereotypes at times associated with young people, i.e. delinquent behaviour, forming gangs, etc., during the interview process for YMAG young Muslims highlighted key topics of interest to them, which included discrimination, identity, integration, extremism and/or radicalisation, foreign policy, education, the media and youth provision. The government's stance on why such a group is necessary is as follows:

> *Creating opportunities to engage with and listen to young Muslims is a key*
> *part of the Government's work to Prevent Violent Extremism. The direct*

*engagement and active participation of young people in the preventing
violent extremism agenda is far more effective than simply engaging with
organisations that claim to represent young people, and is crucial in building
and sustaining resilient communities* (DCLG, 2008).

This implies a change in the direction of how government engages with young
Muslims; however, its coming under the banner of the Preventing Violent Extremism
(PVE) agenda means that it is viewed by some as controversial. A further challenge to
the initiative is created by the government's hints that members of YMAG might be
future community leaders. The implication here is that government is attempting to
influence the selection of potential leaders of the Muslim community, a role that lies
beyond its remit.

Perhaps through such examples of direct engagement government will win the trust
of young people and gain a clearer understanding of the views and opinions of young
Muslims. An open and transparent approach such as this may serve to give this
initiative both longevity and success; time will tell.

Statutory bodies are central in implementing legislation on issues connected to the
well being of young people. They provide education, youth services, counselling, after
school and child care services as well as health and social care, and are invariably a
key component in any policy change. Statutory bodies often feel they are unable to do
all that they wish to and this can be as a result of a shortage in staff and/or financial
resources, which curtail their impact on local communities. Evidence from the
National Youth Agency indicates that youth service expenditure as a proportion of
education expenditure shows a steady decline of 16% from 1996 to 2008 (NYA,
2009). Furthermore, some statutory services will be based in diverse communities
and a reasonable knowledge base of their possible clients will enable them to provide
a more effective and responsive service which is accessed by the so called 'hard to
reach' communities.

As well as government and statutory services, there is one other key audience this
research seeks to address: Muslim communities. Community service groups, both
Muslim and non-Muslim, seek to be the first point of contact with young people on
issues ranging from education to employment, from health care to extracurricular
support and much more. Community groups are often the front line of youth
provision and invest heavily in providing such services; however, whether there is

serious investment in understanding their local community is undecided. Ironically, without the time and money invested into understanding the sensitivities and values of the clients, the community group may often miss the target audience completely. Community resources include faith-based organisations and places of worship, community centres and groups, local community-based initiatives such as sports clubs or initiatives like 'clean ups' of public areas as well as gender-specific projects which seek to empower women.

3
Methodology

One of the striking features of research on the topics discussed below (see chapter 4, 'Literature Review: Young British and Muslim') is that although some attempt has been made to unravel the issues affecting young Muslims, there is much scope for further research. We rarely hear the voices of young people themselves through research; instead we often read of others' analysis and opinions of young people. We tend to hear the voices of those working with young people – academics, youth workers – but rarely hear the voices of experts and young Muslims together. *Seen and Not Heard: Voices of Young British Muslims* has sought to bring these experiences together. In order to understand the challenges young people face in the UK, key stakeholders need to hear from young people directly.

Throughout this research the following types of qualitative investigations were made:

○ Nine focus groups conducted in Glasgow, Bradford, Manchester, Leicester, Birmingham, Cardiff, Tower Hamlets in East London, Brixton in South London and Slough

○ Nine interviews with people ranging from Muslim, Christian, Jewish and state youth workers to young people who are working to support their local communities

○ Secondary research such as background reading and a literature review investigating the existing material that has been published in this arena, conducted throughout the research period of 11 months

○ Attending youth events – conferences, seminars and less formal gatherings – where a variety of topics have been explored and debated

○ Circulation of draft report for comments.

The cities were carefully selected to cover a wide geographical area of Britain, which allowed a variety of voices from England, Scotland and Wales to emerge (in a future project we would aim to include Northern Ireland, but it was beyond the scope of this piece of research) (see figure 1).

Figure 1. Participant breakdown by area

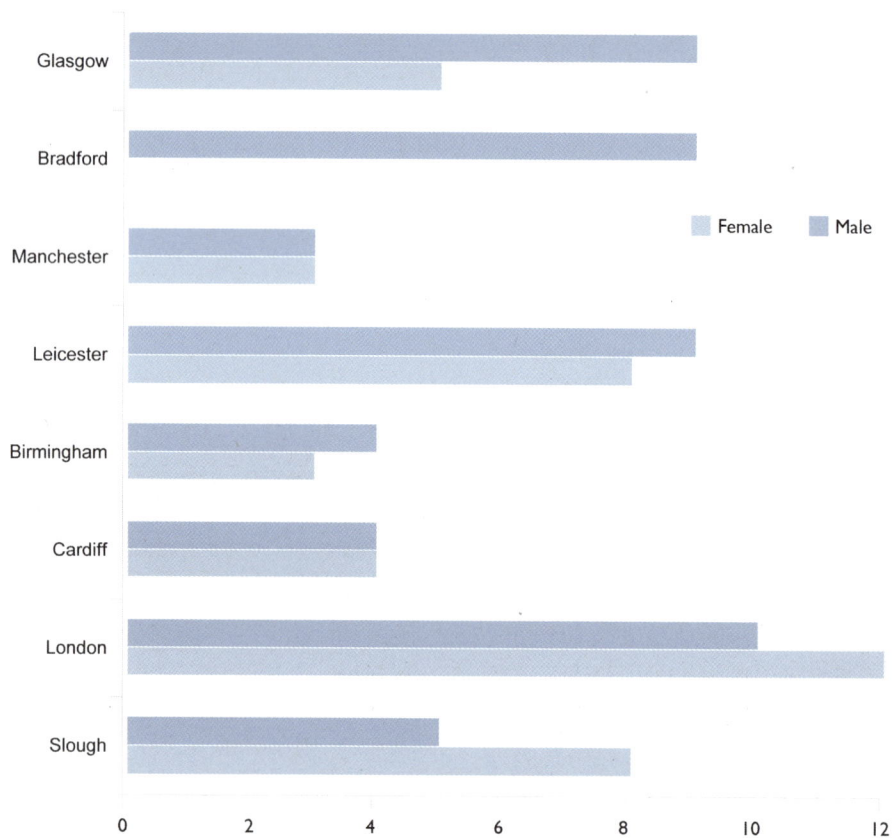

Figure 2. Focus group participants by ethnic origin

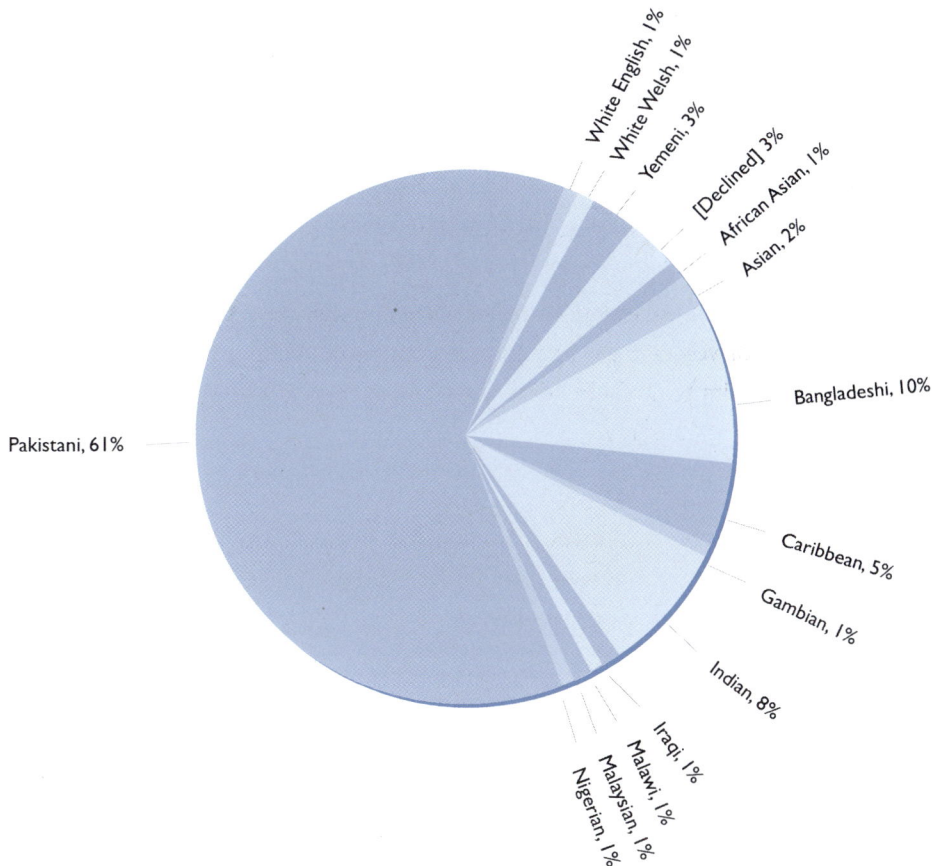

Pie chart showing: White English, 1%; White Welsh, 1%; Yemeni, 3%; [Declined] 3%; African Asian, 1%; Asian, 2%; Bangladeshi, 10%; Caribbean, 5%; Gambian, 1%; Indian, 8%; Iraqi, 1%; Malawi, 1%; Malaysian, 1%; Nigerian, 1%; Pakistani, 61%

Muslim communities are distributed around the country; they are not homogeneous and can often be divided along ethnic and other lines (see figure 2). Therefore it was important for the research to hear from as many ethnic heritages as possible. In Cardiff we found ethnically Arab and Pakistani communities, although Pakistanis, being the largest ethnic group within the Muslim community, were to be found in most of the cities. In Birmingham we heard Yemeni voices, in Brixton we heard from the African-Caribbean community, in East London from those of Bangladeshi heritage, while in Leicester the Gujarati, Turkish and Somali voices were heard. All those who participated had lived all or most of their lives locally.

The focus groups were arranged so that there was a good balance of people aged between 16 and 25, male and female and where possible the participants were an

Figure 3. Focus group participants by gender

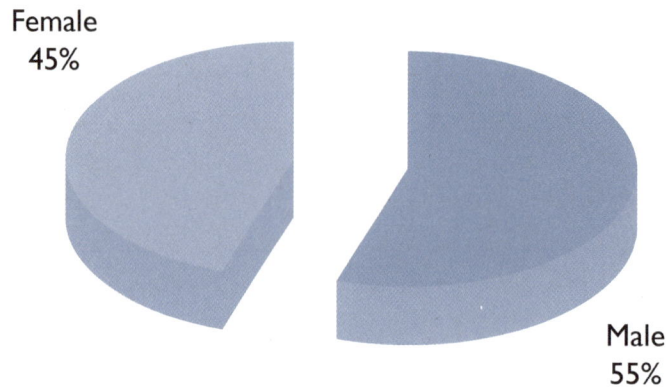

Female
45%

Male
55%

ethnic cross-section of the local communities (see figure 3). This enabled the researcher to gain an insight across many different experiences and helped in creating discussions around the following themes:

○   identity, belonging and citizenship

○   mainstream and religious issues around engagement and integration as well as leadership and role models

○   media and its impact on a young Muslim's life

○   intergenerational experiences

○   listening for other issues young people felt were pertinent.

All participants in the focus groups and interviews were given an introduction to both the research project and the Policy Research Centre; it was considered ethically important to ensure each individual was aware of the motivations and background of this project.

Each focus group discussed the same themes, and debates were centred on these topics so that the researcher had data that could be compared from one region to another. The discussions were recorded so they could be transcribed and included as evidence; this allows the participants to have a direct voice in the report rather than their comments being only interpreted. All quotations have been anonymised to ensure confidentiality.

The semi-structured interviews with academics, youth workers and grassroots youth activists provided a loose framework of questions, which allowed the interviews to benefit from the interviewee's expertise. The interviews also allowed the interviewee to explore and expand on points of relevance and importance. The questions for each individual varied according to their position and experience in the field; nevertheless there were similarities in the content of the interviewee's responses in that many who agreed to be interviewed, although coming from different experiences, shared views on young people and had similar thoughts on the challenges faced by young Muslims. The focus groups and interviews took place over 11 months from October 2007 to August 2008. Those interviewed were:

○   Umar Ansari, Youth and Justice Services Manager, YCSA, Glasgow

○   Bea Foster, youth worker, Burnley

○   Sadek Hamid, Muslim Youth Work Programme Leader, University of Chester

○   Muhammad Adil Ibrahim, youth worker, Glasgow

○   Muhammad Kamran, Hamara Centre & Leeds Muslim Youth Forum

○   Jon Littman, Jewish youth worker, London

○   Shelly Marsh, Director at UJIA Jewish Life Education Centre, London

○   Tafazal Mohammad, Director, Muslim Youth Skills, Leeds

○   Jonnie Parkin, Youth Ministry, Leicestershire

○   Robin Rolls, Director, Youth Ministry, Diocese of Leicester.

It is not the intention of this report to provide conclusive findings which can then be used to generalise about British Muslims; rather, the purpose is to map views and encourage a more open engagement with young Muslims that will allow scope for future research. An important factor in this study is the selection of verbatim quotations, which feature throughout the report and are a means of enabling young people to speak for themselves. The quotations have been selected as the most appropriate and best-serving examples based on a key criterion – their overall representative value from the discussions. These quotes reflect recurring opinions and statements mentioned by many interviewees across the country. Hence, the results of this sample are not representative of the opinions and attitudes of all Muslims in the areas where focus groups and interviews were conducted or in the UK as whole. Instead, they reflect the opinions and experiences of some young Muslims and experts on the subject of youth work based on their own life experiences, knowledge and skills base.

A key part of any research process involves thorough reading and an analysis of existing literature. This project began with an overview of existing material in the form of surveys, reports, academic articles and books. They add to what is still a limited study on young people, particularly young Muslims whom society at all levels is interested in for a variety of reasons, from security issues to integration and assimilation, from identity and belonging to intergenerational experiences.

Finally, there are a plethora of youth events, conferences, seminars and more intimate circles, meetings held on the subject of young Muslims. It is always interesting to observe such events, but more importantly to investigate the themes and topics that have been selected as the focus of attention. While being a more amorphous and imprecise source of data, and usually confined to one city, such gatherings are useful for a general awareness of context, especially the activist agenda in terms of debates around young people.

A roundtable seminar with experts and key stakeholders including policy advisers, youth workers, academics and young Muslims was held to discuss the first draft of the report, which was circulated to roundtable members. Their comments, constructive feedback and experience were debated at the seminar. The feedback from these experts has been used to improve the quality of this report on young British Muslims.

A draft of the report was also circulated electronically to a number of organisations and individuals who were unable to attend the roundtable seminar but had advice and guidance which the report benefited from. These organisations included youth centres, community initiatives, national centres of youth excellence and academic institutes. This enabled the researcher to analyse the findings from the focus groups as well as interviews and compare and contrast them with the outcomes of the seminar.

As the project involved qualitative methods such as focus groups, interviews and seminars, there has been a heavy reliance on people being able to communicate their thoughts, experiences and ideas in an effective manner. This reliance meant that the researcher took steps not to influence participants and to remain impartial at all stages. As the research involved working with people (on an issue that can be regarded as sensitive and even emotive) there was inevitably a risk of subjectivity in gathering data as well as interpreting results. It was therefore important (a) to have rigorous control mechanisms in holding focus groups and conducting interviews; (b) to use multiple methods of data gathering to cross-reference findings; and also (c) to subject the findings to review. The interview questions were formulated with careful planning and word structure so that they did not imply or suggest answers. The interviews were semi-structured in order to allow the possibility of conversation to flow and therefore reduce the risk of restricting the process along rigid lines.

Time limitations play a key role in such research exercises. The project was co-ordinated and researched by one full-time researcher over 11 months, which created a tight working schedule, particularly when national and religious holidays were avoided for the focus groups and interviews. Time limitations often mean the research area has to be tightly defined and focused. This research has focused on specific socio-economic lines and recognises the potential for an in-depth analysis of the variety of socio-economic backgrounds which exist in today's Muslim communities.

This allows for an opportunity of further research in the future, which can focus on the themes we were unable to examine. Furthermore, future research can offer detailed exploration of the key concepts that emerge through this research such as the needs of Muslim youth in 21st-century schools and communities, focused and assertive mentoring, raising attainment levels and transfer of learning from inter-generational experiences of other groups and Muslim heritage programmes capturing the experiences of Muslim pioneers, etc. Policy makers and Muslim communities would find comparative research of young people in the UK and mainland Europe useful to ascertain the varied response of young Muslims to multiple circumstances, for example drawing an investigation into intergenerational experiences and why they may vary from place to place, which is inclusive of the historical backdrop. As well as this, an exploration of the terminology used in association with young people must be visited – how wider debates on radicalisation and the way in which young Muslims are often considered only when issues of extremism concern public agencies is problematic and potentially affects the way young Muslims engage with agencies and communities. The relationship between young people and public services such as the police and educators may benefit from positive language when speaking of young Muslims. Policy makers and the youth work communities would also benefit from research designed to highlight the perspectives of males and females in relation to one another (i.e. is there a difference of opinion on issues such as role models and identity, relations with parents, etc.?), as well as from a deeper exploration of the class divide within the Muslim communities and its impact on young Muslims in majority and minority situations within neighbourhoods.

Future research on the topic of young Muslims could complement this project by utilising quantitative methods to gauge attitudes and perceptions in a more representative mode. Surveys and questionnaires of community-based Muslim organisations would ask questions around the current provision of youth services, and would investigate whether this is in the form of a youth department or wing which tends not to be an integral part of the decision-making body, or whether the organisation was providing youth-led services. National umbrella groups could also engage in surveys to provide an overview of their investment in young people both in the infrastructure of the organisation and the activities. Once collated, a statistical analysis could be drawn which would highlight where youth provision is being made (i.e. does this have a geographical pattern?) and, more importantly, where the gaps in youth services are and how this compares with where a majority of Muslims reside.

Increased funding could help with targeted and thematic research into specific areas such as the effects on young British Muslims of counter-terrorism strategies, discrimination laws and the evolving roles in the family, and their implications for the future. Further study should build on the extensive research and recommendations made in various published reports, e.g. *Muslim Voices* (Muslim Council of Britain, 2005), *Muslim Youth Speak* (Murtuja, 2006), *Faithful and Proud* (Coles, 2005), *Providing Faith and Culturally Sensitive Support Services to Young British Muslims* (Malik et al., 2007) and *Forgotten Voices* (Jawad, 2008) among others.

4

Literature Review: Young, British and Muslim

Sociologists find the word 'youth' has become problematic in that its definition is negative, applying to a phase of life that is neither childhood nor adulthood. Furthermore, young people are often labelled in negative terms, as a group that present a problem for society (Department of Sociology, 2003). This becomes interesting when agencies speak about youth, once they have been essentialised into the 'other', as a delinquent group that doesn't contribute positively to society and undermines the safety of others. Society has in essence created barriers in engaging with young people as well as discouraging engagement by young people. This essentialisation often does not recognise colour, religion or creed; instead it feeds on stereotypes of hoodies, gangs, asbos and yobs, which are generalised to all young people across the UK.

It may be argued that the UK has experienced a rapid growth of subcultures which only young people are privy to. Sociologists such as Brake (1990) argue that subcultures are not created as the antithesis of wider culture or opposition, but instead, as argued by Murdock and McCron (1976), subcultures are an expression and extension of the dominant meaning system, and are not deviant; they rarely become a counterculture (Brake, 1990). For example, the teenage entertainment industry is manifested in youth culture by young people choosing to express their teenage identity through fashion, lyrics, speech and their perception of the world around them. This does not mean they reject wider culture, but that they are part of a subculture, which they can identify with and feel comfortable being a part of. In time it may be that they find an alternative subculture, which suits their adult needs, but at this young stage in their lives they create a subculture, which they can best relate to. Often subcultures are created because young people find contradictions in the social structure which lead them to create a collective identity, one in which they will find like-minded peers who will understand the shared norms and values. This allows an exploration of their identity. Brake argues that this is an exploration of masculinity and therefore relates directly to young men; for girls it is emancipation from the cult of romance and marriage (Brake, 1990, p. ix) from highly developed historical traditions.

Given the nature of political events today, much attention around extremism and terrorism has been focused on Muslim communities of the UK. Research on Muslim communities and Islam has also focused heavily around issues of cohesion, integration, identity and disadvantage. Cities such as Bradford, Leeds and Leicester, as well as small towns such as Oldham and Burnley, have featured in numerous reports and academic writings.

Published material on Muslim youth has investigated the possible explanations for the disturbances of summer 2001 in northern towns and cities, for example reports by Cantle (2001) and Ouseley (2001). Ethnographic research also gives a rich background on Pakistani Muslims in Bradford and other Muslim communities – mainly Pakistani and Bangladeshi – by writers such as Alam (2006), Saeed et al. (1999) and Jacobson (1998). Other research from a religious studies, sociology of religion or history of religion perspective has looked at the development of British Muslim identity (Husain, 2004, and Malik, 2006) and some of the evolving debates within Muslim communities, often touching on the debates around young people (Lewis, 1994 and 2007).

Where research and other published material needs to make a significant contribution is on the challenges young Muslims face and how government, statutory services and Muslim communities can engage better with Muslim youth culture. Some recent projects have contributed to such themes. These include *Muslim Youth Speak* commissioned by the Hamara Healthy Living Centre (Murtuja, 2006) in Leeds, where topics around Islam, education and identity were explored with young Muslims from the city. These people expressed their thoughts on subjects such as what 'fitting' in to society means; they quite clearly saw themselves as integrated young people: "… as

Muslims we have to be good citizens too, try to fit in but not go to extremes such as clubbing" (Murtuja, 2006, p. 25). Others explained how they felt about the incitement of religious hatred:

> *There is new legislation coming out to deport people who incite religious hatred. What are they going to do with the BNP? Because they also incite religious hatred. Where are they going to deport them?* (Murtuja, 2006, p. 29)

Forward Thinking (Jawad, 2008) conducted a similar peer-led project, which explored issues around identity, education and the relationships young people experience with parents.

The implications in the study of Muslim youth seem to be that the problems are endemic, unique and ultimately put us all in danger: 7/7 is the pinnacle of the problem. But is there really a unique 'Muslim problem'? The direction of much of the current public debate and commentary seems to be making the case in the affirmative. It is hoped that this research will help to understand such issues more deeply.

History of youth work in the UK

A brief overview of Church (Anglican) youth provision notes that many dioceses have some sort of youth officer or youth adviser in addition to one or two other youth-related staff; however, it is still considered to be an area of decreasing investment for the Church. Currently there are approximately 7,000 full-time youth workers employed by the Church of England; this is set to increase to approximately 19,000 by 2011. This represents a highly significant investment in youth work given that in 2008 there were just over 6,200 full-time qualified youth workers or youth support workers in 120 local authorities surveyed by the National Youth Agency. When we consider the history of Christian youth work in the UK and its relationship with the state, it is easy to appreciate that despite the targets for the coming years Christian youth work is still playing 'catch up' with the issues young Christians are dealing with. However, some dioceses around the country have employed Directors of Youth Work in order to boost youth-work provision and meet the needs of young people.

The Albemarle Report (Ministry of Education, 1960) was the first serious attempt at understanding youth and youth work; it looked at attempts to get disenfranchised young people back into the youth clubs during the 1940s and 1950s. After World War II, Sunday schools were created as a secondary educational measure and focused on how to teach young people to be morally upright when the schools were closed. Today some Sunday schools have that educational ethos, but as the nature of education and religious tempo of the nation have changed, the Sunday schools have lost their traditional roles.

The madrasah system, through which young Muslims attend a supplementary school for approximately two hours per day, Monday to Friday, could potentially alleviate some of the pressures facing youth workers and youth organisations. Many young British Muslims aged 5–13 years attend such schools to learn a rudimentary knowledge of Islam. Often this learning involves concepts such as prayer and worship as well as learning to read the Qur'an by rote. Some of these supplementary schools are treated as childcare facilities where parents know their children are in a safe space for a couple of hours. Others take a more diligent interest in their child's learning and often support the young person in their learning at home also – similar to mainstream schooling.

Throughout this research youth workers who were involved in such areas complained of the competition they faced for young people's attention, often losing out to computer games and hanging out with friends on local streets; they were generally perceived as an 'un-cool' place for teenagers, particularly, to spend their social time. They commented on the organised structures in the Muslim community such as the madrasah system and its impact on the well being of young people during particularly difficult hours. In policy terms, safe spaces such as the madrasah provide relief for the youth services as well as inculcating positive character and good behaviour in young Muslims. Discussions around character and even 'good' character have recently become interesting to government. The merits of policies and departments dedicated to such concepts in Canada have sparked curiosity in British policy makers. A good madrasah can enhance such debates by providing education centred on Islamic ethics and morality, all of which serve to enhance young British Muslims in the developing of 'good' character, supporting them to become 'good' citizens.

However, for many madrasahs their role is merely teaching the Qur'an (in rote form) and prayer. Muslim communities must recognise the potential which lies in the institution of the Mosque. Should structured and focused syllabi, which aim to instil more than basic reading of the text and prayer, be used across madrasahs it would help to alleviate some of the serious social challenges young British Muslims are now facing.

Young British Muslims under stress

The concerns young Muslims are grappling with require an in-depth exploration in order to appreciate the pressures under which Muslim youth are negotiating the challenges around identity, sexuality, religiosity and so forth. Addressing and working towards creating youth-led service provision has a direct impact on the local communities in which these young people reside. Major obstacles to successful employment and education, and instilling and understanding culturally sensitive norms and values, all play a part in a young person's life and if successful can give a young person direction and guidance at a time when they need it most.

In order to tackle such pressures a combination of youth provision to increase social and emotional literacy and a madrasah education which looks to empower young people should be directly linked to the schools' extended services strand under the new duty on schools to promote cohesion. Developing partnerships between local youth provision and madrasahs as well as schools will enable this joined-up thinking to look at young Muslims as a whole. It will allow clarity of thought and action in how young Muslims are performing, where needs are being missed and primarily will provide constant and consistent care for each child. It will also reduce the likelihood of different messages coming from schools, which may go against the madrasah agenda.

We know many issues challenge young people. According to a survey by Muslim Youth Helpline, the most prevalent challenges for young Muslims were mental health, relationships and religion (Muslim Youth Helpline, 2007). A further exploration of some of these topics is necessary in this report; young Muslims themselves have alluded to some of these issues, and they'll be explored throughout the following chapters.

Evidence shows that young people in the UK as a whole are increasingly suffering from social and emotional disorders.[1] The prevalence of such disorders is thought to be higher in particular family types, and these include lone-parent families where

---

1 Emotional disorders include separation anxiety, specific phobias, panic disorder, post traumatic stress disorder, obsessive compulsive disorder and depression. See Children's Society (2008).

emotional disorders are at 16% compared with 8% for two-parent families, 17% in families where parents have no educational qualifications compared with 4% in those who have a degree-level qualification, and 15% in those living in low-income, high-unemployment areas compared with 7% for those in affluent areas (Green et al., 2004). *A Good Childhood* (Children's Society, 2008 and 2009) marks the completion of *The Good Childhood Inquiry*, by The Children's Society. It provides one of the most up-to-date studies on the subject of mental health and young people in Britain. In a survey of 8,000 14–16-year-olds, carried out by The Children's Society as part of the inquiry, 27% of young people agreed with the statement 'I often feel depressed'. In a separate online vote, conducted by CBBC's *Newsround* for the inquiry, 78% of those who voted said they felt fine, good or really good about their health; however, a worrying 22% felt bad or really bad. Many also said they felt under pressure to look good, with seven out of ten admitting they dieted some or all of the time (Children's Society, 2008).

Many of the participants in the research expressed concern about the impact that poverty and social disadvantage has on mental health and well being. Refugee children, children in trouble with the law, children with disabilities and children at risk on the streets, whom The Children's Society works with every day, are among those most affected by these issues (Children's Society, 2009). A 'mylife microsite' has been set up by the society to understand young people by listening to "what's important to them, what problems they face and what changes would make things better" (Children's Society, 2009).

Muslim youth and mental health

Mental health challenges are not only present in young people, but require culturally sensitive support services from the statutory sector and community groups in order to attract those affected. As we have seen, young people are becoming increasingly affected by emotional and social disorders including depression, feeling 'really bad' and pressurised to look different. Young people seem to be undergoing a state of crisis and as a result are now more than ever in need of well-designed and targeted support from agencies that specialise in mental health, counselling, guidance and providing physical health care. Presently many such agencies are perceived as catering only for those who are under extreme and obvious pressures such as people suffering from anorexia, bulimia, schizophrenia and drug or alcohol-related illnesses. Most young people would not classify themselves in these terms, but nevertheless are in need of support from such agencies. The idea that they are unable to turn to local authority-led service provision further exacerbates the problem in young communities.

Muslim youth also do not seem to approach statutory agencies for such issues partly because they feel the service providers do not understand young Muslims, and also because they do not understand the religion (Muslim Youth Helpline), culture and other norms that young Muslims are faced with within their own community structures daily. Support services that are deficient in such skills are often underused and ignored by young British Muslims who either internalise issues or are unable to recognise such conditions, which left untreated affect both the young person and the community around them. Although precise figures for Muslims affected are not known, the causative factors of mental health and its challenges are becoming clearer.

Space to grow

Some young people in working-class communities spend time socialising with their peers on street corners rather than in their homes, usually because they don't want to smoke or converse in front of their parents; this was certainly the case of the young Muslims in the programme aired on BBC Radio Leicester's *Gangsters*, a documentary by BBC journalist Hasan Patel (Patel, 2007). The young Muslims explained in an interview that they needed to hang around on the streets of Highfields (a predominantly Muslim part of Leicester) because they didn't want to disrespect their parents by smoking cigarettes at home. They didn't know where else they could spend time with their friends after college and as the local youth centre had shut down four years earlier, because of a lack of funding, they were left with little choice but to stand on the streets. Their sense of dress – casual and affordable – was different from their middle-class counterparts in another part of the city, Oadby, a middle-class and more affluent area. Young Muslims in the interviews felt 'hanging around' in groups meant that they were more at risk of being questioned by the local police than their white counterparts in Oadby. As one young man from the Spinney Hills part of Leicester put it:

> *There's no way you can have 10 men in your house… it's a family home… you get bored sitting at home, so you have to come here… the council don't help us out… if you see a group of 15 white people in Oadby they [police] won't see them as a gang but as a group of people, here there's five of us and they see us as drug dealers and in a gang.*

This impression of stereotypes doesn't deal with the problem of young people spending time on the streets; instead it makes them feel like criminals and socio-logically this risks resulting in a self-fulfilling prophecy. If young people feel ill at ease and are made to feel like delinquents or a threat to wider society they could begin to behave in this way and increasingly become detached from mainstream society.

These young people were concerned about the reputation their presence on the streets may be creating – a gang culture because they wear hoodies and hang around in groups of more than two. However, they shared their thoughts on how their presence on the streets could change; they argued that young people in deprived parts of the country deserved more attention than they were currently receiving. They stressed that people should not judge them before they have had conversations with them and got to know them for who they are. They stressed the need for an increase in youth provision which matched the needs of the local communities. In the case of Spinney Hills they argued that a youth centre was needed where young men and women could spend time socialising with their peers without being perceived as threatening to the wider community (Patel, 2007).

Spatial distribution of Muslim communities

The demographics of the Muslim community reflect the proportion of Muslims distributed across the UK. Statistics show just over half of Muslims currently reside in London with Birmingham and Greater Manchester following behind (ONS, 2001). These communities often live in the most deprived parts of the cities. Those who have settled outside the largest cities tend to settle in clusters which can be seen in Bradford and Kirklees, etc., often in the most socio-economically deprived areas.

Small towns in the north of England are reflective of these demographic patterns also as local authorities' recent investment into 'facelifts' reflect. Regeneration in places such as Oldham, Blackburn and Burnley is focusing on the most deprived areas first; often these are inhabited by significant Muslim communities. The pattern is a reflection of the socio-economic imbalance; they can afford to live only in some of the poorest areas in the country. These are issues of primary concern for government policy, statutory services and community groups as studies have shown the strong links between socio-economic deprivation, educational underachievement, poor housing and poor health – all of which directly impact the 3% Muslim population in the UK by virtue of the fact that an overwhelming majority of them live in these socio-economically deprived parts of the country. This directly impacts on the socio-economic future of young people in these communities; studies have also linked outcomes in health, income, housing and education to such living conditions.

In response to the picture painted above, several organisations have sought to fill some of the gaps in youth provision. For example, the Muslim Youth Helpline (MYH) has grown rapidly since its inception (August 2001) and has tailored its operations around areas such as counselling – both via telephone and the internet – as well as campaigns like the 'Prison Campaign', where small boxes are sent to Muslim inmates during Ramadan. These packs are usually sponsored by the Muslim community and contain messages of support and encouragement to work towards a positive future. They also contain a prayer mat, sweets, a Qur'an, and an Eid card for inmates to send to their loved ones. MYH offers a service which statistics show is in great demand; the MYH website is full of information on the situation of their young Muslim clients. However, the service is London-centric and a strong case can be made for a MYH in every major city in Britain.

Other responses to the current gaps in youth provision for Muslims include the Muslim Youth Work Foundation (MYWF), which operates from the National Youth Agency offices in Leicester. Since its inception in 2006, the MYWF provides e-newsletters periodically advertising and raising awareness of youth-related projects, funding, courses and activities around the country.

The Muslim Youth Helpline (MYH) is a registered charity that provides pioneering faith and culturally sensitive services to Muslim youth in the UK. Its core service is a free and confidential counselling service available nationally via telephone, e-mail, the internet and a face-to-face befriending service in the Greater London area. The service uses male and female volunteers trained in specialised support skills to respond to client enquiries.

The Muslim Youth Work Foundation (MYWF) is currently working with young Muslims to reduce the gap between community need and service provision by enabling young people to take advantage of youth-led schemes. In particular, exchanges and trips with young people of any background to help broaden the understanding of British youth of cultures and experiences outside Britain has been a feature on the MYWF e-newsletter.

The MYWF is an innovative national Muslim youth work organisation that places young people at the heart of its purpose and function. The MYWF is unique in its ability to integrate different types of youth work, which is reflected by a board that brings together a range of experience and expertise.

Schemes such as the Glasgow-based Youth Counselling Services Agency (YCSA) are grappling with a fast-paced environment in which they aim "to enhance the capacity of young people, individuals and groups" in their communities. This service caters for young people in and around Glasgow, although an interview with Umar Ansari (Youth and Justice Services Manager) revealed that they are rarely able to meet the demand they have on their time and resources from the minority communities of Glasgow. Muhammad, a youth worker, explained the motivation behind YCSA:

> *There wasn't any counselling service targeting ethnic minorities or understanding their needs, so we set up from that, and there were a number of things that had happened around about the mid-nineties in our school that I think also had an effect on how people felt… There were things like a riot at the local secondary school involving quite a lot of ethnic minorit[y] young people, specifically Muslim young people, who basically raided this school for the death of Imran Khan, a young boy who was killed and the effect that had on [this community]…*

YCSA clients range from Pakistani to Chinese, Indian to the African-Caribbean communities and the range of issues they approach YCSA with are diverse:

> *It could be anything from family problems to drugs-related problems to anger management, whatever it may be, religion in school, issues in school with their education; so for example someone from the drugs and alcohol team, they might get a young person [to] come, and they will need support in counselling; the majority of drug and alcohol users need some level of counselling. On top of that they might not have something to do in the evening after school/college so we provide that service. On top of that they might have left school with pretty much no or very minimal education so no literacy and numeracy which would provide the basic skills required.*

The services of the YCSA are designed to enhance the capacity of young people, individuals and groups within communities. It is responsive to demands and offers support services, on-demand training and positive, friendly staff responsive to individual and organisational requirements. It specialises in youth work, counselling, support, learning and advocacy.

The YCSA specialises in several strands of work – youth work, learning, advocacy and counselling – which enables it to provide a holistic support service for its users. Unfortunately due to a lack of funding it is unable to continue catering for its clients as effectively; recently it lost some funding and it is unable to resource appropriately skilled staff and premises. Projects such as the YCSA rely on local government funding as well as support from the local community – Muslim and otherwise. Staff explained that they were unable to take half a day away from work to attend an important meeting related to research on young Muslims as they had recently lost several members of staff and were under an immense amount of pressure.

Faith and youth work: divergent points of view

Sadek Hamid from Chester University and Tafazal Mohammad, a member of the Advisory Board for Chester's BA Muslim Youth Work and the Director of Muslim Youth Skills, respectively, reflected on the challenges they feel are not currently being met in the landscape of youth work. They also expressed support for Muslim youth work rather than youth work generally, arguing that young Muslims face extra challenges, which require understanding and support beyond that which youth work generally can offer them. A different view is held by Bea Foster, a youth worker in Burnley, who argues against faith-based youth work and explained that it can isolate young Muslims more than they currently may be.

Many grassroots organisations work with young people vis-à-vis community projects including away days, summer camps, study programmes and various other sports-related activities throughout towns and cities in Britain, some local and others national. Groups such as the Dawatul Islam Youth Group and the Young Muslims UK are examples of organisations that run many youth-related projects taking place through grassroots Muslim organisations, which deliver projects and offer opportunities for volunteering in many British towns under the directives of faith-based organisations.

The Young Muslims UK (YMUK) began in 1984. It aims to provide young Muslims with the space to learn about, understand and practise their faith, with an emphasis on the British context. It relies heavily on volunteers and its activities include sports; raising money for charities, conferences, regional camps across England and Scotland; and the use of new media to link members across the country. The organisation seeks to provide a reliable source of information on subjects around faith, identity and citizenship and education; it provides a safe place to explore such topics in a relaxed environment while mixing with other young British people.

These groups, although working actively with young Muslims, do not necessarily conduct 'youth work' in its formal sense. Often the lack of capacity, training and resources allow them to provide only general activities for young people. They bring together a range of professional skills from other sectors to voluntary services, thereby providing a form of social capital through a limited scope of youth services without burdening the taxpayer. When speaking to staff in such organisations it was very clear that although they saw a need for youth work with Muslims, they recognised the fact that they are not professional youth workers.

Instead they saw their contribution in creating safe and secure environments for young Muslims who identified with their organisation to explore their faith and identity as well as to learn new skills such as camping and survival skills. This type of work with young people is popular among such organisations, and is often the only contact a young person may have with other young Muslims from different parts of the country. At times it works as a spiritual invigoration and at other times as an academic learning opportunity about Islam and British Muslims. However, given that most young Muslims are not members of such organisations and do not attend such events, there is a wide scope for formal youth work to take place – this is indeed a necessity for young Muslims. Youth workers and academics such as Sadek and Tafazal argue that there is a growing need for youth work in the Muslim communities, and that Muslim youth workers are best able to fulfil this need.

In contrast, Bea Foster, a local authority youth worker in Burnley, discussed the challenges of being a state youth worker, a practising Christian and working in the heart of the Black and minority ethnic (BME) community, of which the majority is Muslim, in Burnley's Daneshouse and Stoneyholme. She was transferred to Burnley after the disturbances of 2001 and has since worked in the same community with a vigour and passion for working with young people which attracts them to community-related projects, enhancing their prospects and enabling them to value their worth. Bea has a very clear understanding of youth work and its challenges:

> *The stance which I've always had in my youth work practice would be that Muslim young people are young people who are Muslim, not Muslim and then are young people. Do you see the subtle difference? And I think that's a lot to do with the fact that, rightly or wrongly really, I find Muslim young people feel very much under attack, and they feel very much that their identity is under attack, and that people want them to lose their identity as Muslims and want them to just become English and not have any of their own cultures and stuff like that.*

In her experience the key to successful youth work is to see young people as young people first; other layers to their identity come later for her as a youth worker. Bea's description of how young Muslims are feeling and understanding their identity in Burnley suggests that young people have many layers and facets to their identity; however, society, and at times the media, pushes them to understand they are different, which essentialises them as a 'foreign being'. She adds that this process "is feeding the pre-conceived ideas and the prejudice of the indigenous community".

In line with the hearts and minds theory of youth work, some youth workers consider their work as:

> *made up of body, mind and soul, because that's what we're all made up of… the work that I do with young people is in some ways all those things, around looking after the body, about being healthy, it is all that stuff around the drugs, the eating, the drinking, about how you abuse your body, or you don't and you look after it very much so. The mind is about education, it's about learning, it's about knowledge, it's about information, you know, your mind is learning all the time. And then your soul, it's about that spiritual aspect of life, which is around reflection, it's around thinking; it's around values and all of that sort of stuff.*

This helps us to think of young people as multi-dimensional so the strategy should be adapted to serve people from different religions and cultures, or from a background of no religion and so on.

A former youth worker from Oldham expressed a serious issue of discrimination he had witnessed within the youth work sector:

> *There's lots of limitations and I actually had encountered some problems in terms of expressing my faith or practising my faith and in short basically the senior management structures in Oldham were very hostile to religion in general and it seemed Islam in particular and that's a pattern you may be aware of, an Islamophobic undercurrent; it's become more covert now but it's still there. The fact of the matter is, when you're talking to young people and you're working with young people, and it's been the case really since the late eighties, religion is a very important part of their lives; whether they are practising or not it's a primary identity.*

It is disquieting to learn that such issues exist within a sector that has been created to protect its constituents, particularly in the case of youth work. A strong sense of trust and reliability is required between youth workers and the young people they serve and any type of perception of discrimination makes it very difficult to build trust and loyalty. Youth work can have an extensive influence on a young person's life, and an effective youth worker, as we found in Burnley, is not only trusted by young people but is also a valuable resource for the local authority in creating a cohesive and harmonious community.

In support of this, Downes (1966) argues that subcultures emerge "where there exists an effective interaction with one another, a number of actors with similar problems of adjustment for whom no effective solution as yet exists for a common, shared problem". This theory is applicable to young people across the world who have similar challenges of adjustment, as we see in the case of young Muslims who struggle to understand their place in the world (as all young people do), but as well as this struggle, they try to grapple with negative notions and stereotypes of Islam and Muslims. They find themselves negotiating the personal world they inhabit as well as the dynamics of wider social interaction and engagement.

Young Citizens in Birmingham has a six-year track record of organising young people around quality of life issues and has developed an 'active citizenship' teaching programme for schools, to be taught as part of the 'citizenship' curriculum. It is guided by research such as listening campaigns and aims to address, through action, issues that threaten individuals, families and neighbourhoods. In the spring of 2003, Young Citizens launched the *Saltley Inquiry* by going door to door to talk to over 300 people about how they viewed problems and challenges in the community (Young Citizens, 2003).

5
Education

One of the most shared experiences for all young people is education, Coleman (1961), along with Brake (1990), makes an interesting distinction between the current social system and one for adolescent society. He argues informal status determinants are constructed, e.g. 'messing around' in class, sports for boys and appearance for girls in opposition to formal goals in secondary school. As Sugarman (1967, p. 168) alludes, norms for the non-conformist include smoking, truancy and dating as well as fashion and music; these tend to carry negative stereotypes, which reflect on the young people of this subculture, which in turn influences the way they are treated by teachers and peers.

Other studies argue that these subcultures are governed by class, then family and then neighbourhoods. Murdock and McCron (1973) argue that middle-class pupils are more engaged in their education and may merely dabble in delinquent norms such as underground subcultures. They argue that "class inequalities penetrate deeply into their everyday lives, structuring both their social experience, and their response to it" (Murdock and McCron, 1976, p. 18).

The argument that class has created divisions across British society has a legacy throughout the history of the British Isles; class is entrenched throughout communities and across cultures far more than in other western social systems, i.e. the USA. This class divide makes it easier for young people to create subcultures which fall in line with the external class stratification system, so young working-class people could naturally incline towards anti-school attitudes, group solidarity and opposing authority, as argued by Brake (1990, p. 62):

> *Youth itself is not a problem, but there are problems created for example by the conscription of the majority of the young into the lower strata of a meritocratic educational system, and then allowing them only to take up occupations which are meaningless, poorly paid and uncreative. Working-class (youth) subcultures attempt to infuse into this bleak world excitement and colour, during the short respite between school and settling down into marriage and adulthood.*

He adds,

> *School values are seen as effeminate; masculinity is celebrated through the tough manliness of hard, unskilled, manual labour. The very values which help the 'lads' cope with school, are the same ones which ensure their entrapment in manual labour, just because they reject school.*

The low expectations are reflective of the low achievement young working-class communities experience in education, statistics consistently echoed by the underachievement of young Pakistani and Bangladeshi boys – until recently the highest underachievers at school. Recent statistics show that this pattern is changing. The Joseph Rowntree Foundation (Cassen and Kingdon, 2007) found:

> *Nearly half of all low achievers are White British males. White British students on average – boys and girls – are more likely than other ethnic groups to persist in low achievement. If they start in the lowest categories of achievement in primary school, they are more likely than other ethnic groups to remain there at the end of secondary school… Boys outnumber girls as low achievers by three to two. But the gender gap is larger for some ethnic groups – Bangladeshi, Pakistani and Black African – among those not achieving any passes above D.*

There are specific groups of young British Muslims who are especially vulnerable to underachievement and low-level engagement with educational institutions, for example care-leavers, recent arrivals to the UK and other recent migrants as well as a more complex group of Muslims who are in a cycle of poverty passed from one generation to the next (similar to economic deprivation in sections of wider British society). All share similar challenges, which undermine their engagement with education.

Although "low parental education levels generally lead to low achievement levels among Pakistani and Bangladeshi children" (Khan, 2008, p. 27), there are signs of positive school performance, as Khan explains:

> There are some areas where the figures give grounds for hope. In particular, the intergenerational cycle of deprivation that affects many White British communities is less pronounced for Muslims. Aspiration levels of many Muslim parents for their children are often very high, even when parents have low qualifications or low paid jobs themselves. Many schools have reported that where Muslim children are attending a poor performing, majority White school, they raise the aspiration and attainment of the whole school (Khan, 2008, pp. 21–22).

The educational process, as well as providing learning for young people, is also an opportunity for parents and young people to engage with public services. However, both young people and the experts interviewed consistently implied that the relationship between the young person and parents became fragile and continued to break down as the parent and child became distant from one another during a young person's school life. Youth workers interviewed argued that the educational system changed frequently, so much so that a young parent or older sibling may not recognise systems such as examinations, subject choices and other assessment methods just a few years on, and therefore are unable to relate to them. Frequent system changes make it difficult for parents and young people to engage with each other and with the school system; quite often young people are left to their own devices with parents feeling left out in the cold:

> My mum can't keep up to date with the new changes in education, 33-period week, and changing to intermediate from standard grades, and it's so complicated they don't even understand… and they even change basic grades from 1234 to ABCD. My mum can't keep up and my dad can't keep up either!

Young Muslims in the UK are largely from a working-class culture with the majority of Muslims living in neighbourhoods considered to be the most deprived wards in

England (Khan, 2008, p. 38) and often are reflected in statistics as underachievers, anti-school rather than pro-school and generally displaying signs of disengagement with school authorities. Often their parents are ill informed of the young person's progress or lack thereof and tend not to have strong relationships with the teachers and/or school governing bodies. The focus groups reflected this situation across the country and young people related their own experiences of parents and school:

> *They [parents] don't really support the kids, they don't take an interest in what they are doing in school… it's like they don't really care whether they do well or not.*

The research shows that attitude, language, poor education background and feeling insecure with systems of school governance can turn parents away from helping children with their homework, coursework and other assessments, remembering that many parents of the first generation didn't attend school in the UK and in fact have a generally poor track record of education themselves. This also discourages them from gaining closer contact with their child's teachers through parents' evenings, meetings with teachers and award ceremonies. If the parent is not fluent in English, or finds it embarrassing to speak in English, then frequent changes to the syllabus, examination methods, assessment criteria, and the choice of subjects and courses serve to further isolate parents. Coupled with potential anti-school subcultures, this adds to the intergenerational experiences pulling the young person and his/her parents further apart:

> *A lot of parents probably don't actually know the language and don't actually know the structure of this society. They actually put the pressure on the children to ensure they are actively engaged in school so if they come back with no GCSEs or really poor results, well, next thing what they're gonna do for them is actually tell them off and put them through the education system again, without even trying to help the situation. The next best thing to do is to say ok get a job as a taxi driver or in the restaurants and we'll get you married off and that's what usually happens as well.*

> *It shows that when there are parents evenings at school as well, a lot of Asian families, their parents won't turn up because they just, I think that they just can't be bothered listening, they'll just tell them we can't turn up because we've got a problem.*

Building on the existing communication between the educational institution and parents will serve to counteract the perceived defeatism of parents. The communication must be a genuine and sincere attempt at raising awareness of the challenges a young person faces in education and the impact a positive parent–child relationship can have on the young person's life, both in the immediate and long-term future. This type of interaction subsequently increases the opportunities for the young person to succeed, which directly impacts on their choices in life. A close trilateral (parent–child–school) working relationship may not resolve all school-related challenges for young people, but it can help to develop a pro-school culture through better and regular parent liaison. Many schools have recruited parent liaison officers who work with individual parents or groups of parents to build their confidence and capacity in supporting their child through school. Some parents may have a negative attitude to school; however, most want to engage but have no mechanism to do so. One way of engaging these parents is through parent groups – an active drive to increase Muslim parent governors and provide support for parents in understanding the school system. The new duty on schools puts an onus on schools to 'know their own communities'; they are required to conduct regular parent and wider community audits to better understand needs, and then through extended services help address those needs. This quality of the home learning environment is critical for whether a child is successful or not in school. Early years provision take up is particularly poor among Muslim families and needs to be addressed if Muslim children's attainment levels are to rise. Khan explores the role of education in the lives of young Muslims and comments on the direction he envisions: "One third of British Muslims are under the age of 16 compared with one fifth of the population as a whole. As a result of this younger age profile, education policies aimed at children and young people will have a disproportionate impact on Muslim communities" (Khan, 2008, p. 26).

When asked about religious education, particularly how young people felt about their experiences when growing up and learning about religion, most young people said they were sent to mosques or madrasahs after school each day for one to two hours. A minority were taught at home by parents (much like home supplementary schooling); however, none of the participants had grown up without this experience. Nevertheless, when asked about 'education', they associated the word with formal school, college or university life rather than the services provided by madrasahs and mosques.

On the whole the quality of supplementary school provision requires dramatic improvement. While this is an important aspect of education for Muslim children, it does mean that they are limited in attending after-school activities. It is important that where Muslim children are not attending extracurricular activities because of the need to go to Qur'anic classes, the school and the madrasah or Arabic teaching institution work closely to look at complementary timings. This will mean children have the opportunity to attend all activities as they see fit.

In terms of the supplementary provision, Khan suggests it is "a good idea to bring supplementary schools closer to mainstream provision in order to raise the quality of teaching in both and ensure that the effects of attending time-intensive after-school provision does not have a detrimental effect on general educational standards but actually helps raise standards" (Khan, 2008, p. 32).

Further research should explore the impact of supplementary education – religious or otherwise – on young Muslims: is it time efficient? Are these young people feeling too tired for compulsory teaching at school during the day? If so, what can the teaching institutions do to alleviate pressures on these young people?

We have discussed madrasah education and its impact on youth work and related agencies, but what happens to young British Muslims once they no longer attend the mosque or madrasah? Most participants argued that life throws many challenges at them and therefore they are busy contending with exams, choices for college or university, relationships, fashion and friends – similar to other young people. Religious practice is not something they seem to have much time for. However, more than half of the participants shared experiences and anecdotal evidence which shows that post 9/11 and 7/7 Muslim youth have increasingly become conscious of their religious identity by virtue of the fact that everyone around them is discussing Islam. Over and above the negative backlash on the Muslim community since the terrorist attacks, young Muslims have felt that the wider community is watching and scrutinising both Islam and Muslims. The realisation that they didn't know very much about Islam (except that which was learnt in the madrasah) meant they were unable to explain Islam to those around them and in most cases this factor seemed to compel them to learn about their faith.

Critically, participants in the focus groups reflected that this learning was devoid of cultural habits endorsed by their parents and/or grandparents over many years. This now presented new challenges to their households in that the young began to question the elders by comparing what they had discovered in the sources of Islam with what their elders believed. This situation occurs in a range of issues from forced marriages to seeking higher education for girls. Although the male participants shared these experiences it was the females who were particularly vociferous in discussing the topic of education and where it can lead. They argued that their parents' expectations of them and what they understood as their rights and responsibilities as a Muslim were, at times, at polar opposites. This juxtaposition means that young Muslims have found it difficult to negotiate these realities in their own minds, which has at times led to disowning what parents advocate as Islam, constant battles about topical issues or leading double lives where they come to an acceptance that their parents have a cultural understanding of the faith and are not going to change that traditional thinking.

A long-term solution may lie within trilateral partnerships between madrasahs, youth groups and schools at a local level; this is critical in maximising the time young Muslims spend in each of these three areas. This type of joined-up thinking could harmonise better the identities of young Muslims, which are often negotiated internally – each of these institutions adds to a young Muslim's identity in different ways and collaborative working will enable them to understand their role in a holistic fashion rather than creating split identities which are expressed differently depending on the institution they are attending.

Despite the recent changes in trends of underachievement, education remains a key challenge for young Muslims and Muslim communities more broadly – not just in terms of achievement but in the wider range of issues in the area. Those who do become successful will often leave the inner-city areas in which they grew up, creating a 'brain-drain' as well as a drain in cultural and social capital. As we have seen, the role of parents in the schooling of children is also an important debate that Muslim communities do not seem to have grappled adequately with yet.

A further observation is that with the differential in school attainment between boys and girls in a relatively small community, anecdotal evidence seems to suggest that it will have a serious impact on career ambitions, outlooks on life and even marriage choices for the younger generations.

The mobility of young people can become an important factor in further education and professional development. However, in the case of Muslim youth, it appears that due to cultural and family constraints, reduced mobility, especially for girls, may have an impact on educational and career development prospects. Young people within the Muslim community often have obligations towards the family structure that could be more complex than their non-Muslim counterparts. As a result of enduring notions of the extended family, leaving home seems difficult for a young person unless the transition is for an essential job, or for setting up his/her own family through marriage. It has gradually become more acceptable for young people to move away , however the preferred choice is still quite often for the individual to commute to a local institution rather than leave home.

Young Muslims 'in learning' will benefit from work-based learning schemes offering information, advice and guidance and possible routes into employment. Currently many young Muslims feel such services are ineffective for them either because of service providers reflecting a level of detachment from a religious and/or cultural understanding of the challenges and opportunities young Muslims are dealing with, or because of a lack of awareness of the public pressure and constraints perceived by young Muslims, which often create barriers for them when seeking education and employment.

Muslim youth in the community, often young people who are not in education, employment or training (NEET), require access to information, advice and guidance outside traditional means of learning such as schools and colleges, particularly in the case of young Muslims who are not registered with any agency, but have particular needs which require culturally sensitive support and access to the same services that their counterparts 'in learning' may benefit from.

Education also plays a key role in setting up the framework for social cohesion and integration, which will be explored further in the next chapter. Culturally mixed communities at school level are uncommon in most inner cities. Certainly the focus groups reflected such dichotomies:

> *I was gonna say I reckon it's about the way we've been brought up for example all the schools that I went to. In our school there are mainly Asian people. I went to school with him and we're the same age and we've been to same school all our lives. The schools we've been to, there's probably like 3% non-Asian.*

You go to school for instance like [omitted]. I had the experience to go there. That's the other way around, it's like 98% white and 2% Asian.

That's the problem because… if you had a mix, say 50/50, at least then integration is made easier, it's easier to mix, it breaks the barriers then.

A stronger engagement on a social level requires further development whereby young people from different backgrounds spend time getting to know one another in a natural setting. This process of building cultural exchange and experience is a multi-agency task. For example, the School Development Support Agency (SDSA) in Leicester is currently looking at how twinning of schools with a majority BME student population and a majority white population can help build cultural competency among pupils. The twinning of schools was an idea suggested in the *Community Cohesion Report* (Cantle, 2001), with the aim of working with young people while they are at primary schools as they are more responsive to change and their views will shape their futures.

But this research stresses the need for social interaction in a natural setting, which will have greater impact and longevity. Young Muslims in the focus groups commented on the deliberate nature of community interaction, but argued that they come from communities within which the majority population is Asian and/or Muslim and they therefore find the same people at such events. Young Muslims need social and community events, and funding for the provision of youth programmes should be allocated in order to create mixed interactions between different ethnic groups, inclusive of both genders. Creating intercultural dialogues is a new strand of thinking for policy makers. The aim of such initiatives should be that all neighbourhood funding, especially directed to the young, must have the principles of intercultural and intra-cultural dialogue underpinning their funding regimes.

6

Identity, Belonging and Citizenship

People challenge British Muslims that you're either British or Muslim; why can't we be both?

Since 9/11, and to some extent since the Rushdie affair, debates centring on Britain's Muslims have ensued across popular and political spectrums alike, on topics such as loyalty, belonging, citizenship and identity. Feelings of allegiance and faithfulness are complex notions to grasp; contemporary debates link these to discussions on how we understand when an individual has a sense of belonging to a community and understands their rights and responsibilities as a member of that community. Such questions are often asked of those who may be considered to be recent arrivals, migrant communities and, since 9/11, young British Muslims. Young people by definition are often at a stage where they are trying to understand their place in the world and when – faced with complexities around identity, belonging and citizenship – they find it problematic that they are being asked to define who they are to the wider British communities. Often those who ask such questions have a perceived identity of young British Muslims, which is built through preconceived ideas and at times typecasting, which has led to racism, an experience shared by a young man from Glasgow:

There were some kind of roadworks and there was this old woman… walking towards… she started walking faster… and as soon as she walks past us she goes, 'This is my country, not yours.' We stood there and we waited for her to go past! Now really, us, we were in school back then, so if it was someone younger, I'm not going to deny we would have probably started... but it was an old woman. What could we say to her?... It wasn't because I didn't have anything to say; I can have a mouth on me when I want, but if I did start saying something to her then, the rest of the white people walking up and down that street would have thought, 'Young Muslim mob attacking an old woman.' It would have been on the headlines and everything!

As well as facing questions and challenges to their loyalty young Muslims (and other young people) today are living in unprecedented times both in terms of globalisation and the popularity of new media. They are also facing complex concepts such as being pressed to define their identity in light of national and international events that are instantaneously transported across the globe, pushing young Muslims to provide explanations and answers for the actions of others. The burden of proof that Islam is a peaceful religion and that Muslims are law-abiding citizens is often placed at the door of young British Muslims. Not only will this at times fail to reach conclusive answers, it is also unfair. This is especially damaging when myths and stereotypes surmount accurate information, resulting in young British Muslims being portrayed as a threat to the well being of the wider British communities.

Questions around identity, belonging and citizenship are closely related and often overlap in discussions with young people. In such dialogue examples of other societies are often referred to, particularly those of Bosnia and migration within and beyond the Indian subcontinent; for example, first-hand experience from elders:

From Professor Anwar's paper, we see that 60% of Muslims in Britain were born here and they now represent the second and third generations. I am from the remaining 40%. But I was born a British subject in India where it became unsafe for me and my parents to reside so we sought sanctuary in the then East Pakistan. We learned the language, the customs and the culture but eventually we were told that we were not loyal and so we had to leave. We made our way to England nineteen years ago. Now again I am asked are you loyal and do you belong to this country? (Seddon et al., 2003).

Young Muslims often hear examples of when communities have integrated into society and feel a sense of loyalty to their country, but feel it is rejected by the wider society.

However, many young Muslims feel comfortable with their British identity and at times are confused as to why questions around citizenship are circuiting British society. Some have argued that loyalty lies with their religious values, which are in unison with their national identity as their faith strongly encourages allegiance to the nation state, so they are governed by the law of the land and are answerable for their actions in the same way as their non-Muslim counterparts are. Some have argued that loyalty is derived from feeling involved in the shaping of national identity as opposed to living in a climate of exclusive nationalism which most may reject (Seddon et al., 2003). Throughout his research for *Made in Bradford*, Alam (2006) noticed "that yet again, here was a group or type of individuals being talked about, not being talked to. Alongside this absence of real communication, a demonisation of this 'type', and indeed a wider ethnic group, was continuing to develop." By becoming the designers of their own identity young Muslims feel empowered and engaged in the process which often has young Muslims at the heart of its debate.

The complexity and dynamism of the debate includes layers of multiplicity in stories of migration, identities and histories, both pre and post migration. It is certainly further complicated by the focus of the media and other agencies attaching labels, implying Muslims are a foreign being within our borders and becoming obsessed with young Muslims and their views on international affairs, which often results in making young Muslims feel confused when their British identity (feeling British rather than being accepted as British) is questioned in public domains. The way in which some Muslim communities and individuals (especially young and male) are portrayed and perceived suggests that a construction of an alien, or at best insular and distinct, culture is taking root. In *Made in Bradford* Alam (2006) goes on to explain: "Now, more than ever, British Muslims are asked to prove themselves as not only loyal and peaceful, but also as integrated citizens." Due to the major changes in policy and political outlooks coupled with dramatic global events, British Muslims today find themselves in the midst of interconnected debates touching on immigration and nationalism as well as citizenship and integration. However, the 'miniaturisation of people', a reduction of the complexities involved in understanding and appreciating a community, as coined by the Nobel Prize winner Amartya Sen, potentially has a long-term damaging effect by ignoring the "intricacies of plural groups and multiple loyalties" (Sen, 2006, p. 20) of the multicultural British Muslim community.

Peers seem to have the greatest influence on young Muslims; the desire to be accepted by others like them overrides other influences:

I'm saying a person is mainly influenced by his friends because does he spend more time with his family or at school? If he skives he is going to be at school with his friends for 6 hours of the day 5 days a week he's away from his family. Saturday, Sunday he wakes up, comes down, has breakfast, he's gonna go back to his friends again, so most of the week he's with his mates. Whatever his mates are gonna do he's gonna be doing the same thing, so if they're all smoking pot in the corner he's gonna be smoking.

Similarly if peers are involved in learning or employment it acts as an influencing factor on other young Muslims who often aspire to be like their closest friends, subconsciously taking them to be their mentors.

Young Muslims told this research they feel engaged in society, describing their engagement in their own words. There is an overarching sense of a need to engage, which was a common sentiment expressed in the groups, but this appeared to be borne out of a responsive need within the context of contemporary issues. Less easy to determine is whether the stimuli for a need to engage has resulted in a greater connectivity between Muslim youth and civic belonging. While a responsive attitude was a common factor among participants, the responses themselves are indicative of more diverse thought trends. Muslim youth are probably more politically literate and aware of global issues than their peers because recent events have forced them to be. Therefore Muslim youth are not choosing to remove themselves from the mainstream democratic system but the system is perhaps unwilling or unable to listen to their views of 'dissent', deciding to label this as disloyal. However, Muslim youth may not be alone in feeling they are being unheard but, worryingly, may be the primary group that is being scrutinised for their response to this.

Young Muslim women in the Brixton group, predominantly of African-Caribbean background, felt they were among the most engaged members of their local societies, even when they compared themselves with Muslim communities in other areas of the country. Such determination was expressed by these young women who customarily wore plain black coverings, over their faces in most cases. A key basis for their view was the lack of cultural baggage, which they felt held back other more typical (Asian) Muslim communities whom they perceived to be culturally entrenched rather than religiously conscious. It was a strong adherence to an ethnic (usually Asian) culture that was seen to be an obstacle to integration.

Others in Scotland argued that a return to tradition could be the way forward for some of their peers. Young people in our study reflected on ideas such as arranged marriage, respect for parents and other 'traditional' values, which play a strong role in many Muslim families. It was somewhat surprising to hear that arranged marriages were now being sought by the young people; they were turning to their parents and asking them to arrange their marriage – often abroad. When probed further, the young people expressed that they had seen many such marriages work and keeping their parents happy was a key factor in their own happiness; therefore arranged marriages were seen as a positive step rather than an act of oppression or compulsion. Of course this differs from a situation where the young people involved do not wish to marry the person of their parents' choice (forced marriage), but in this scenario it was the young people who were actively pursuing such lines. Is this because they have seen a generation before them who are waiting longer than is traditionally the norm before they settle down into married life, or perhaps they have seen the increasing number of people who find difficulty in locating a suitable partner, or observed breakdown in families?

This viewpoint presents a stark contrast with the female participants of the Tower Hamlets focus group where girls vocalised how difficult their parents' cultural traditions had become for them as young British Muslims. In confidence they explained that they had 'been economical with the truth' to their parents about where they were going that afternoon because any social or 'mixed' (with the opposite gender) activity was disapproved of by their parents. They would also go against their parents' wishes when the subject of marriage arises; should their parents wish for them to marry abroad through an arranged marriage they would do everything they could to dissuade them.

In Brixton, the picture of a religious group connected through their faith and positive local experiences was echoed by the male participants. Those experiences depended on the space within which they could live an ideal of a 'true' Muslim life. Any negative intrusions within that space would affect that sense of solidarity which would impinge on their understanding of their identity as young Muslims from Brixton, the majority of which come from a convert (or as they termed, revert) community. Their views tended to be more conservative than other focus groups and their conviction of the idea that they are practising young Muslims and engaged within British – or at the very least Brixton – society was balanced by the idea that should anything hamper their way of life and they are unable to live in this way then migration to a 'Muslim' country would be an option:

> *[As] Muslims we are supposed to migrate to a place where it is Islamic and this country is not an Islamic country.*

The young person expressed this opinion on the basis of a particular understanding of Islam:

> *So yeah, the reason why… obviously because we believe we are supposed to be in a Muslim country that's what makes us feel like… you know, technically we are not supposed to be here. We should be in a Muslim climate but we were born here.*

Such dichotomies presented by individuals can also be seen in wider debates and are often presented to young people by some activist groups. While religious sentiments yield a sense of connection, it was still an intra-perspective, that of a circle within a larger square. There was a perception of a set of norms within society, but these norms had, necessarily, to be pushed out of the circle. Engagement here, then, was equated with feeling 'comfortable' rather than civic representation. It was here that a sense of agitation was expressed that "no one is trying to get to know us", that on sight of the black veil people "automatically assume you can't speak English" and, when pressed, that "exceptions are made for other people".

According to participants in Brixton society called for Muslims to make fundamental concessions to religious teachings and the vast majority of other Muslim bodies, representative of parts of the Muslim communities, had done just that. Participants were convinced that government funding for local projects, including for the Prevention of Violent Extremism, required a compromise to such fundamentals. They complained of the violation of fundamentals in social aspects, pointing to the use of musical instruments in audio material and the 'mixing' of males and females. One participant asserted that inquisitive young minds fell into two camps: those who fell for the compromises, and those who were agitated by them and their claim to represent Islam. The 'liberal' or 'sell-out' Islam being purported by the Muslim media, Muslim organisations and the mainstream media is doing a disservice to young Muslims in that they are now faced with two extremes.

1.   The Extremists. Young people participating from Brixton felt characters such as Abu Hamza and Abu Qatada were given far too much time and space in the media, which contributes to radicalisation, especially in institutions such as prisons:

> *A lot of the extremism comes from non-Muslim media outlets as well. I mean they might see a Bin Laden video or Abu Qatada speech on the BBC of all places and say that we are trying to combat extremism and the Muslim community is not doing more to help and they are making the problem ten times worse by giving these people a platform to speak on. Do you know what I mean?*

Things become even more challenging when young people look for an alternative to the likes of such extremists, and in this case young men felt:

> *There is no organisation representing the youth. What they are doing in authority in most of the cases they are chasing the youth away so that Abu Hamza comes and says look they are trying to dumb down Islam.*

2.   The Sell-outs. The second extreme was identified as the 'sell-outs' who represent large groups within the British Muslim community but compromise on key issues which the young people of Brixton feel are at the heart of Islam, such as dress, music, shaking hands with the opposite gender, etc.

Such examples are perceived to be unrepresentative of a true practice of Islam and therefore such young Muslims either feel further disillusionment with authority and representation or become confused as to why it is these two extremes that represent Islam in the public domain. The notion arising here that there is no organisation that genuinely works for young Muslims, however much this may be contested, shows that there are important fractures in Muslim communities that have not been bridged. This is also compounded by a sense of inner turmoil in feeling rejected by society:

> *I was born in this country and I have rights, I obey the law yeah and why should I be made to feel like this really, you know I'm an outcast, I did something wrong because I am a Muslim?*

Foreign policy and sense of belonging

In Slough there were marked differences in what the participants believed was the agenda behind the war on terror. In a clear disagreement between two participants, a case was made for the 'war on terror' being a war directly on Islam, against the case of a war dealing with a scourge that Muslims did not subscribe to. Both participants felt they represented the majority view of British Muslim youth, though they recognised the subjective nature of their positions. The holder of the former opinion felt a strong sense of connectivity and allegiance to Muslims overseas, in preference to Muslim and non-Muslim British citizens. This preference, according to the claimant, was embedded within the teachings of the Muslim scripture (the Qur'an), and was, for the participant, not an area of negotiation. Although the use of terrorism was not condoned, the cause of such acts and the blame was squarely put down to historic and contemporary issues of modern foreign policy. One participant added that "had it not been for pro-integration groups such as the Islamic Society of Britain, I could have been attracted to the easier [more black and white] message of an extremist group", in the search for identity and belonging.

While debates around loyalty were driven by an ongoing war (Iraq, etc.), where a sense of national belonging was acknowledged but effectively overridden in terms of concerns overseas, such belonging was harder to ascertain in the view of participants in Brixton. So while there was also a closer affiliation with people outside Britain, the grounds are different. One participant argued there was nothing 'holding' her in Britain, and so she felt 'no connection'. This was a measure in her mind of the cultural norms and religious beliefs of mainstream Britain, and its distance from the notion of Islamic religion (influenced by Saudi religious thought). In both cases, participants often spoke in terms of 'them and us', even though they may have used them differently, and were often unaware of this until probed further; even if it was surprising to some.

Identity and belonging: false 'choices'

Much like other young people in general, young Muslims also feel a sense of tension when it comes to questions around national identity, particularly those in England. By contrast, their Scottish and Welsh counterparts feel a strong sense of identity in being Scottish and Welsh and when questioned further they reluctantly disclose a sense of Britishness, but their affinities lie with Scotland and Wales. These feelings and attitudes are reflected in wider British society and are symptomatic of the complexity of British identity.

A very small number of young Muslims confidently expressed their Englishness and in fact became confused by the question of identity: "Why am I being asked such obvious questions?" When the researcher explained that identity and loyalty were topical issues which the wider British public was trying to understand, the young people explained they had only ever known England and understood themselves to be English and British. Scottish Muslims feel Scottish, but this became problematic when we discussed how they are perceived by other Scots. It was generally agreed that the majority of Scots would not understand Muslims to be Scottish, but in the one scenario where a young man did feel others saw him as Scottish, it had a strong impact on his understanding of himself:

> *Scotland beat Italy, and the day of the match I was in town, and that day was the first day I ever felt properly Scottish. I think there were four or five white people drunk out of their nut and I was on the train, and one actually came up to me and he put his arm around me… and said, 'Do you know what guy? You better be supporting Scotland today.' I said, 'Of course I am.' He said, 'I'm going to buy you a flag.' I said, 'Why?' and he said, 'Because you're Scottish too.' And that's the first time I've ever felt properly Scottish.*

The group in Cardiff, by contrast, had far fewer tensions in accepting a sense of belonging. They were British, and felt it:

> *I feel, genuinely, we do try our best to engage… from being brought up in Cardiff… I do think, yeah, most Muslims from what I see… do try to engage.*

> *I went and studied in [nearby] Swansea and there was a distinct [difference], you know, they were completely segregated, it was like their own community, as Muslims… they were segregated from the non-Muslim community, even, I suppose, there was a distinction between the old and the young.*

The presence of a 'with it' mosque imam, who was instrumental in creating an inclusive and relaxed atmosphere at a popular, local mosque and its community youth centre, had clearly helped the youth adjust and negotiate their multiple identities. Almost all young people in this group said they would use their Imam as their most trusted port of call for religious questions. Female participants mentioned they would ask the imam's wife in the first instance. When asked why they did not go directly to the imam they responded they could if they wanted to, but usually asked his wife. A notable feature was the blend of ethnicities. The ethnic diversity and a Jordanian imam meant the chief language of communication was English, which enables greater communication between the imam and young people, making him potentially more approachable and trusted by his local communities. The participants in Cardiff were acutely aware that their environment was not typical of most Muslim communities in the UK, and clearly valued the local imam. They referred to nearby Swansea as a place that was not as lucky, and alluded to problems of socio-economic challenges:

> *The valleys has a lot of socio-economic problems and I think that has quite a lot of influence on the way that non-Muslims perceive Muslims and the way that Muslims interact with non-Muslims, and I think it's mainly due to the poverty and that kind of thing; I don't think you can underestimate the impact that that kind of thing can have…*

However, as for participants in Brixton, there was a strong local sense of independence with little real connection or experience of other locations. How they viewed other Muslim communities was, ironically, based on portrayals in the media.

In other parts of the country it was argued that being British and feeling a sense of integration for young Muslims was different from what was considered to be integrated by their white counterparts. The young people in the focus groups explained that, for them, feeling part of British culture meant a feeling of engagement whether that be through employment in a variety of sectors, education for those at college or university or the social activities they were involved in such as campaigning for the environment, animal welfare and poorer communities. They explained that even though they may not be as interested in what was often deemed to be aspects of 'youth culture', e.g. clubbing, drinking, etc., that doesn't take away from their sense of Britishness and integration. As one young man in Slough made clear:

> *When I go to school for example, I wouldn't do the things that a lot of them are doing, like drinking, going out. These sorts of things aren't really typical of a young Muslim to do, be it because of religious reasons or our families or*

the culture that we come from. Whatever the reason is, we aren't really engaged at that sort of level so I guess you could say detached from that sense… But we're involved in other levels, I think that it's really broad, you can't just paint everyone with the same brush really…

Other sorts of belonging: class and political action

It is interesting to note that there seemed to be a class consciousness in the minds of young Muslim participants; they came from the poorer parts of British society and were clearly aware of their working-class identity. When discussing community involvement in maintaining good neighbourhoods, getting involved in causes which affect the whole of society, some felt this is where the responsibility of the more affluent Muslim community lay:

How many Muslims, it's not even us, like if you think about Muslims who call themselves a certain class or whatever – how many of those take part in issues like the environment, Greenpeace and animal rights and stuff?

Although they desired to make a change in the world, some couldn't envision making that difference directly themselves, they saw such causes as being outside their sphere of influence. Those who did participate in causes that affect everyone did so through established organisations that work in grassroots communities. Through such vehicles some of the young people had been able to become more involved, which increased their sense of social responsibility, knowledge of the issues they were campaigning for and greater self-awareness. The roles they played enabled them to understand their own likes and dislikes better as well as discovering where their skills and talents lay.

Frank and open discussions

The challenges young Muslims face often require frank and open discussions on topics that may be controversial and possibly sensitive. Cultural taboos often inhibit such discussions, which forces young Muslims to either repress their experiences and concerns or speak to other peers who are ill equipped to deal with the challenges. Research by the Muslim Youth Helpline highlights the top five issues which their clients face, as shown in Figure 4:

Figure 4. Helpline users by age

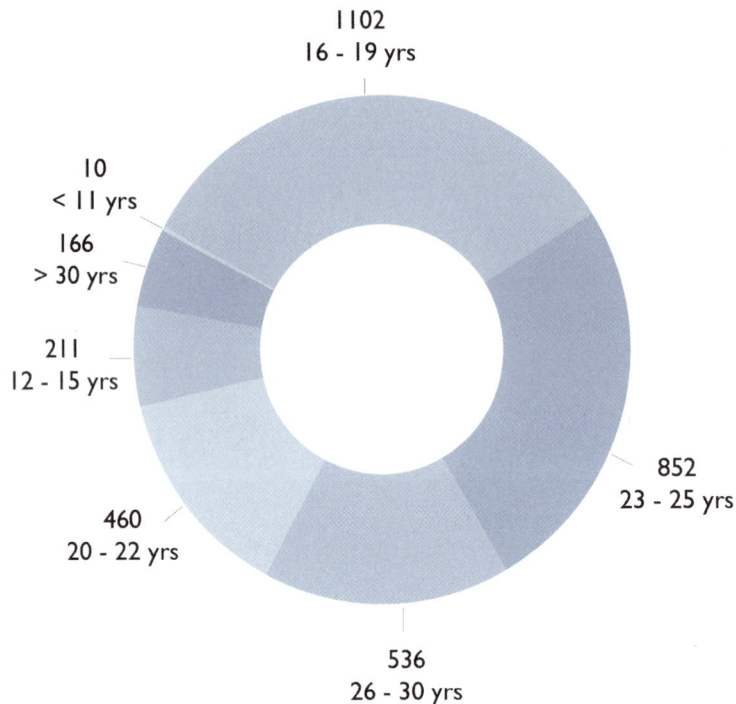

1102
16 - 19 yrs

10
< 11 yrs

166
> 30 yrs

211
12 - 15 yrs

852
23 - 25 yrs

460
20 - 22 yrs

536
26 - 30 yrs

○ relationships

○ mental health

○ religion

○ offending and rehabilitation

○ sexuality and sexual health (Malik et al., 2007, p. 26).

Although MYH statistics show that 58% of their clients are from London, they are becoming increasingly known and trusted in other parts of England; 26% of their client enquiries are from the northwest of England, despite having no physical presence and London-centric advertising. This is a strong message from the young people in the northwest region – a reflection of their needs and the desire to contact those whom they perceive best served to deal with the issues, in this case not their local authorities or local community groups, but a Muslim helpline in London.

Young people in the focus groups openly discussed the challenges they face in their localities. Discussing issues around relationships with parents was not considered to be a viable option because of the religious and cultural barriers they felt existed between parents and their children:

> *For something like that you wouldn't talk to your parents because, alright, at the end of the day they are your parents but it's that respect at the end of the day.*

> *I feel awkward going home and saying, mum this happened today with this girl I met, whatever, you'd feel awful wouldn't you…*

Although respect, religion and culture were the key reasons why young Muslims would not look to their parents for discussions on some of the topics that concern them, they also highlighted an added dimension which prevents them from fully engaging with their elders, the intergenerational gap:

> *I think 'cos with the generation gaps a lot of parents have actually come from abroad… are actually still [in] traditional ways, some of them haven't learnt the language for example so what usually happens is sons and daughters who have virtually now grown up in the English society have now taken over… so the parents leave it to them to make their decisions…*

The young men argued that there is a visible gender imbalance in treatment from parents, which means boys and girls in the same household are treated differently to such a degree that it affects their life chances. Interestingly, the young Pakistani men were the loudest in voicing these concerns:

> *The Muslims, the majority of the Muslims in Bradford are Asian right, Pakistani, they don't give girls the chance. That's what I think. They don't give girls the chance as much as they give the guys to go out and take part.*

Our research showed that discourses on identity, loyalty and belonging were varied across the country and across Muslim communities. While the expected issues of tension such as foreign policy (and government policy more broadly), being treated in a hostile way and aspects of social life such as 'pub culture' did arise, the vast majority of young people who spoke to us felt no contradiction between their religious and national identities. They felt part of British society and wanted to be treated as equals, not to be privileged, nor discriminated against. This negotiated aspect of their identity and how they locate themselves in society also came across as something that is in creative flux – it is constantly being redefined in light of politics, access to global and new media and the influence of peers and community.

7

Community Leadership

Role models and peer-mentoring

Role models for young people often tend to be in the form of fashion icons and celebrities from the world of music and acting, as well as sports stars, particularly in football. Young people often look to those in positions of success and seek role models to help develop their aspirations and potential for the future. Particularly for a community whose parents were mainly unskilled labourers, positive role models are an important factor in creating encouragement and hope for young Muslims.

The Diocese of Leicester provides a good example of how the Church is responding to the changing needs of young people. The city has an innovative project called 'Church for young people, by young people', which aims to educate people about accepting leadership from young people. Some of the challenges include working in a world where a traditional Church of England congregation may be more interested in liturgical modes in which people read scriptures, but the words read may be alien to some young people who live in a world of Facebook, Skype, YouTube and msn, which are all IT-based, visual, instant and experiential.

The British Scouts Association is a further example of young people coming together to gain skills and learn more about who they are. The Scout Association describes its work as follows:

The Scout Association provides adventurous activities and personal development opportunities for 400,000 young people aged 6–25. Internationally, we have over 28 million young people enjoying the benefits of [our services] across 216 countries. Personal development means promoting the physical, intellectual, social and spiritual well-being of the Scouting individual, helping them achieve their full potential. In Scouting, we believe that young people develop most when they are 'learning by doing,' when they are given responsibility, work in teams, take acceptable risks and think for themselves.

By offering young people such opportunities they are able to harness the potential and talents of young people; through such a process they contribute to creating leadership and role models that can help their peers.

The impact of role models on youth development is understood widely; positive role models can at times be the most constructive thing in a young person's life, both emotionally and psychologically. Often role models can encourage young people to develop strong aspirations and in this way they can be guided to make informed choices and better judgements about a variety of issues such as education and career paths, but also relationships and peer pressure. Role models are often used as sounding boards also; a young man in Bradford spoke at length about the changes he experienced in his life once he had developed a sense of trust with his role model. He benefited by having a trusted source to approach when questions around his faith, identity and relationships arose. The psychological impact of having 'someone to look up to' often means young people can find guidance and advice which they feel is meaningful and pertinent to their situations; this can create a feeling of empowerment as well as an increase in confidence and self-esteem.

Importantly, discussions with young people reveal that they often seek role models from within their communities, Muslim communities need to identify positive role models so that young Muslims are able to look up to those who come from similar backgrounds and have faced similar challenges and succeeded. Such role models help young people to have a genuine admiration for those who have become constructive and successful members of society – often despite their circumstances. This will be a sign of a confident and well-functioning community that can create and respond to aspirations.

The notable absence of serious leadership for young Muslims has had an impact on the youth growing up across Britain. Young Muslims often look to sports personalities such as Amir Khan and others as role models. Unfortunately there are very few Muslims positively represented in the public eye and this is a vacuum which needs to be filled in order to provide hope and aspirations to young people.

The Muslim communities of Britain have yet to create a sufficient quantity of leadership figures that are respected by grassroots Muslims and at the same time can deal effectively with the political challenges of the day. A number of important organisations exist at the national level which represent Muslim voices to government and policy makers; others have come and gone. In the focus groups, when speaking with young Muslims, many were unfamiliar with any of these organisations and among those who were, a number of voices felt inadequately represented. This poses a problem in the leadership of the Muslim community and by extension the role models for young Muslims. However, others have argued that there has been a steady growth in Muslim organisations that engage with both government policy and Muslim communities; leadership is a natural and gradual process, which must be supported and not undermined. They argue that every organisation has something to offer and many are engaged with different strands of the Muslim communities; however, they find themselves limited in time and resources.

Today there are initiatives for working with young British Muslims which are both innovative and effective. Projects such as Mosaic, led by Business in the Community and the Prince's Trust; the Young Muslim Leadership Programme established by the Oxford Centre for Islamic Studies and the Prince's Charities; the Leadership Development Programme organised by the Muslim Council of Britain; CEDAR (Connecting European Dynamic Achievers & Role-models), a newly established pan-European Muslim professionals' network, launched in partnership between Institute for Strategic Dialogue and the Salzburg Global Seminar – all four programmes attracting young Muslims from across the UK – are significant measures which are being taken to develop tomorrow's leadership and skilled voices across the Muslim communities. The emergence of leadership from within the Muslim community is a real potential, and given time and support from Muslims and others will inevitably grow. Online presence, such as the Emerald Network, has also created valuable spaces for Muslims of diverse backgrounds to interact, network and connect. In order to respond to the pressing and immediate needs many more initiatives such as those mentioned may be needed.

Intergenerational experiences

Leadership in many of the traditional Muslim communities has retained a sense of the *biraderi* system (traditional Indo-Pak tribal system of social order) in which kinship and age are important factors. The traditional tribal hierarchical system is criticised by many young Muslims; they argue that respect and honour should be gained through diligence and hard work and not given because someone is older or of high ranking in the caste system. Many young Muslims feel disconnected from such structures and look to other forms of leadership, often to find few figures within the Muslim community who both understand young people and appreciate the challenges they face as they are growing up.

The gap between young Muslims and their parents is, on the one hand, similar to that of their peers in other communities and, on the other hand, considerably different from their non-Muslim peers. Some face issues which include being unable to talk to their parents, parents unable to relate to their children and therefore finding it challenging to provide advice or guidance at the appropriate times and parents generally being perceived as out of touch with young people. As alluded to above, this shared experience was vocalised both by the young participants in the focus groups as well as in the interviews conducted with those who work with young Muslims, Christians and Jews.

For a community recently formed through migration, cultural barriers between generations are also very significant as they compound the intergenerational experiences and tensions. Young Muslim participants argued that there was a large gap between them and their parents; this was attributed to several factors. Most parents either spoke English as a second or third language while others spoke no English at all. Young Muslims, however, have been born and raised in an environment where English is their first, and sometimes only, language. When the preferred language of communication is one that is not shared comfortably by both parent and child obviously this will have a significant impact on the quality of communication. Young Muslims across the country said that they could communicate at their best and with confidence in English and no other language. There was also the issue of street slang, which subconsciously enters speech; this creates an invisible barrier between young people and their elders who prefer their children to speak a language such as Punjabi, Urdu, Bengali, Arabic or Gujarati when communicating in the home. Therefore when young people find it difficult to articulate their thoughts and feelings, there is an added pressure in that they cannot communicate with their parents for fear of embarrassing themselves in their 'native' tongue or for fear of not being understood by their elders. Naturally, this creates a barrier to meaningful discussions about the more sensitive issues that young Muslims are concerned about.

Challenges in parent and child relationships include barriers between the two due to the inability to communicate effectively, and current taboos on topics such as relationships, mental health and education – religious and otherwise – all contribute to young Muslims often leading parallel lives: one within the home and the other beyond the family and community ties. Often taboo subjects fall outside such a domain. The overarching poor socio-economic conditions further impact on such difficulties as parents (particularly fathers) are sometimes forced to prioritise work over familial commitments.

Due to such challenges, some British Muslims can be uninformed of their heritage and the experiences of their elders as well as religious teachings, which can often confuse and even create space for misguided knowledge of their religion. A safe space in which to learn and understand such topics potentially serves to counteract extremist and radical interpretations of Islam as well as enabling British Muslims to appreciate their past, giving them a clearer idea of their future roles in British society. Some young Muslims were asked what would encourage young British Muslims to feel more confident and engage with community structures:

Young person   *First of all give them a better understanding of their own religion so they know what they're about and why; it's like if you call yourself a Muslim and a non-Muslim comes up to you and asks you a question and you don't have an answer it's gonna put you off, full stop.*

Interviewer   *So stronger religious education?*

Young person   *Yeah it's like we need a proper religious education not a 4–6 madrasah where they go and learn the Qur'an.*

Interviewer   *What would be 'proper'?*

Young person   *It's like where they have classes within the schools in English for instance or any other language and they learn about their own religion.*

Young person   *I know about a couple of years back we used to go for 2 hours play football for an hour and then have like an Islamic class for an hour and in that we used to have food as well. That was good.*

Such activities have often been arranged by voluntary groups that often unable to sustain such projects on a long-term basis due to a lack of resources.

But 'generational' gaps aren't necessarily always between grandparents, parents and children, they can be more subtle. Robin Rolls (Director of Christian Youth Ministry in the Diocese of Leicester) talked about:

> *Generation X who grew up in the Kylie–Jason era and had a link with faith that then connected them to a sense of identity. Compare this generation to the next generation, known as Generation Y. These are young people who are now growing up with faith as a leisure option.*

Clearly more research is needed to evidence this and look into it further, but initiatives within the Church are responding to these perceived changes and attempting to deal with the challenges they bring, especially at a time when young people seem to be absent from church on Sundays. Robin Rolls argues:

> *Young people are in this sort of strange tension, they are of course driven by such marketing and consumerism on the one hand and then demonised by the language used to describe them: yobs/hooligans/lads etc. If you read the media, they are the ones who vandalise property, rob old ladies and scare the 'law abiding' public.*
>
> *Young Christians however are referred to in kinder terms: they raise money for charity, help with community events and so on; they are not known as 'youth' but instead 'young people'. Language labels young people from whatever background they come from.*

This difference between the ways in which young people are portrayed in the media will be addressed further in the next chapter.

The importance and utility of mentoring and peer-led support mechanisms came out very strongly in our research. While good steps have been initiated in this direction much more can be done to build capacity among young Muslims. Young people require the support of statutory agencies, Muslim communities and government in order to make their contributions to British society. They require economic and skills-based support to develop their own talents, which in turn can serve to benefit their local communities. Beyond this, there is also a need to look seriously at the intergenerational experiences of young Muslims and how communication and relationships can be enhanced.

8
Media

The reservations young people have about the media, often relate to the way in which the media tends to profile and depict youth. We frequently hear them labelled as 'hoodies', or the 'ASBO generation', and the use of the Mosquito (piloted in Burnley) exemplifies how young people are stigmatised in society (discussed in the chapter on policing and crime). However, examples of young people as portrayed in the media do not correlate with how young people perceive one another. The media is reputed among young people to be sensational and distort the truth about them. Examples of young people in mainstream media often stereotype the way in which young people dress. This terminology has now become synonymous with young people. When headlines are about hooligans, yobs or gangs they are naturally associated with young people in the mind of the reader.

Young people in our research said they are often misrepresented and stereotyped in the media:

> I've seen loads on [the television and newspapers] how young people go around streets and yobs and the asbos and how much under-age drinking there is, and how much drugs they use, I never hear anything good about how young people are doing.

One youth in a focus group mentioned that Post 7/7, young Muslim men were paid approximately £50 each to stand in front of a mosque or the Hamara Centre in

Beeston, Leeds. These pictures were then used in newspapers and on television news bulletins representing a scene that was not natural; rather, it was orchestrated.

For some young Muslims the media is seen to be extremely influential and is at times discussed in quite defeatist terms. Comments such as 'they don't want to listen to anyone so what's the point?' and 'you can't really make a difference' are heard among Muslim youth, referring to both local and national media. Television, radio and newspapers are seen as uninterested in getting to know young Muslims. Frequently stories of extremists and/or terrorists are reported using terminology that links with young Muslims and overtly with their faith. A young participant from Glasgow explained: "In *The Scotsman* paper they were saying: 'Muslim this, Muslim that', – in every paragraph and every sentence they had 'Muslim' in it. You know, it was like targeting Muslims." Some young Muslims in our focus groups argued about the absence of consistency when reports, news and stories of people of other faiths often do not mention the religious affiliation of the perpetrator(s). They questioned the integrity of the media, and although they acknowledge all media are not the same, they felt that media agencies operate as businesses looking to make money rather than aiming to inform the public. As one young man in Bradford put it: "I think it's a big money-making thing", and others agreed that the media reports that which serves its purpose and should the readership continue to be interested in something the media will prioritise such themes and stories: "If people don't read it, it wouldn't sell." Others however felt that although the media continued to behave in a manner that young Muslims feel intimidated by, it also does inform public opinion, though even this was pictured in negative terms:

> *It's like the audience that watches the news and reads the papers yeah, they are like blank pages just waiting to be written on basically the media is so stereotypical it just fills... Everyone's heads (a second male said, finishing the sentence off).*

Others argued that although some say the media is anti-Muslim or anti-Islam, an opinion which more young Muslims had in common was that "It doesn't like anyone" and therefore Muslims are no greater a target than any other community. The reason the Muslim community was featured so frequently and consistently in a negative fashion was because "something happened and it got an audience". It wasn't planned but as the subject attracts great attention the media is going to continue covering Islam and Muslims in this way. Some young people argued against the portrayal of their community in this way. Others, although they felt a blow to their confidence and self-esteem, argued that this inaccurate perception was pressurising them in an unnatural manner in which they cannot be themselves but instead feel the need to express opinions, get involved in social projects, and learn more about their local community and their faith, all of which under 'normal' circumstances would be a far more gradual and 'natural' process. This type of behaviour makes them feel they constantly have something to prove: that the negative stereotypes and judgements others make of them are inaccurate:

> *So kind of putting them in a box in a sense and [judging] them all by the same sort of [stereotype]. 'If you have a beard you're like this, you're like that.' And I wouldn't just say it's the elders or the older people that are doing that, I would say that a lot of people my age would have perceptions like that simply because when they turn on the television they see all these images that are blasted onto them, like; this is the perception, this is what it is and it's painting Muslims in a really negative light I think… media in general.*

Most of the young people differentiated between different types of media: TV, radio, print; local and national; and online and new media, and also felt that there were complex factors as to why some were more aggressive in reporting and coverage than others. Interestingly, some people reflected on the impact of the negative portrayal of Islam and Muslims and argued, both in England and Scotland, that: "All that stuff, it doesn't put me off, it motivates me to go out and be more involved, to make a difference."

Most young Muslims in the focus groups saw it as a challenge that they should rise to and proactively counteract the negative perceptions of themselves and their communities by talking to their non-Muslim peers and allowing them to get to know Muslims first hand rather than through the media. They also consciously made an effort to become more vocal about their religion and take steps to find religious teachings in order to become more informed about the subject, noticeably because they felt a sense of external pressure with so many questions about Islam and Muslims. However, others thought the media was too powerful to work with and felt threatened by the way in which it provided a platform for extremists. They argued that this would undermine cohesion and create barriers and obstacles to integration:

They see one Asian person's mistakes, and the rest of the community, the whole of the other Asian population has to pay for it.

There's obviously some kids who are growing up… young white teenagers that are growing up now… since they were born, as far as they can remember, [throughout] their teenage years… all [they've heard] about Muslims are terrorists, Muslims are terrorist, Muslims are terrorist. And by the time they're at an age where they can physically do something, they'll have so much hate inside them for Muslims, that whenever they see anybody, they're like: 'That person, he's either a Paki, or he's a terrorist, or they're here in our country.'

The tense relationship between the media and young people requires exploration as to how better dialogue can take place as well as highlighting positive examples of where media has been both responsible and effective. Further research would need to investigate the relationship between Muslims and mainstream media and how myths surrounding the media and young people can be debunked. The lack of engagement of Muslim communities with bodies such as the Press Complaints Commission and Ofcom means that when Muslims feel aggrieved they may not always trust, or even be aware of, the processes in place to channel their critical feedback, opinions and frustrations.

On the other hand, as a result of the negative portrayal of Islam and the fact that young Muslims often cannot identify with such depictions, many young Muslims have been encouraged to learn about their faith. They feel motivated by the perceived challenge from the media in counteracting the stereotypes and myths surrounding their communities. This has created an artificial situation where young Muslims feel a sense of pressure and a burden to comprehend the teachings of Islam so that they are able to answer others who question them as well as deal with extremist messages coming from fringe groups, often when they do not have the experience to do so, or may have other priorities in mind.

9

Policing and Crime

Through the discussions in the focus groups and interviews, the research looked at young peoples' sense of personal liberties and confidence in local policing. Has their experience of civil liberties changed in recent years and if so, in what way?

Young people have developed a reputation of 'hanging around streets' and one of the most controversial choices of managing this presence has been the trial of a deterrent called the 'Mosquito'. The Mosquito is a device that can emit a piercing sound which can only be heard by young people – similar to devices used to scare animals – and is aimed at dispersing groups of young people congregating in public spaces and suspected of 'being a nuisance'. Civil liberty groups have argued the Mosquito has breached the civil liberties of young people across the country. With the gradual disappearance of safe spaces for young people such as youth clubs and youth centres there has been a natural spillage onto other public spaces and young people often spend time socialising with friends outside the home. There are few alternatives where they are able to be themselves without the pressure of parents, teachers, community leaders and so on.

We heard the experiences of young Muslims and the way they feel targeted at times by authorities such as the police. Suggestions by young Muslims on how this could change and how barriers for effective engagement could improve were offered by a group in Bradford: they will communicate and participate "if they know their voice is going to be heard".

Young person	*Yeah if they know that someone is going to pay attention.*
Young person	*I don't think it's that – 'cos like this area alone there is like one here and there but there's nothing going on for kids. For us lot though [16–25 year olds] there's nothing for the weekend to go outside or anything else and like it's up to them ain' it [to do something about it].*
Interviewer	*What kind of things would you want to see on the weekends and in the evenings? What would you want to see from these organisations?*
Young person	*Youth centres.*
Interviewer	*Youth centres that do what? What kind of activities?*
Young person	*Take kids out on the weekend, teach them.*
Interviewer	*Teach them what?*
Young person	*Life skills… life skills as well for instance survival, to me that's an exciting thing.*

Similar sentiments were shared by young Muslims in Leicester when they were interviewed by a BBC Radio Leicester journalist (Patel, 2007). As mentioned above, they argued that the closure of youth centres meant they were forced to congregate on their local streets to spend time with their friends as they did not consider their family home an appropriate space to socialise.

Strong feelings were also aired about anti-terror legislation and its impact on Muslims. Some argued that Section 44 of the Terrorism Act 2000 allows the police to stop anyone at anytime without reasonable suspicion (Wilson, 2008). Although some records show that young Muslim men are stopped disproportionately, the Leicestershire Constabulary's information page (Leicestershire Constabulary) clearly states the police have powers to stop and search individuals only when they have 'reasonable suspicion' that one of the following is being carried on the person: drugs, weapons or stolen property and items which could be used to commit a crime.

Young Muslims were keen to share their thoughts on how laws such as stop and search had affected them. Their understanding of the Terrorism Act 2000 was that the police have the power to stop any individual whom they feel is behaving in a suspicious manner. As explained above, police require 'reasonable suspicion' before stopping and searching people; however, this is contested by some grassroots communities who feel they are being targeted by police officers without good reason, and guidelines to stop and search are being breached by individual officers. Throughout the research there was a consistent element of distrust of the police and examples were given of young people being targeted and harassed by officers. They argued that this method of policing infringes their personal freedom and sense of security; instead of feeling protected by the police, they feel they are threatened. Between 2001 and 2003 there was a 302% increase in 'stop and search' incidents among Asian people, compared with an increase of 118% among white people (Home Office, 2004).

Young men in Bradford discussed anecdotal evidence of their experience with the local police and one person explained: "A lot of Asians especially after the Bradford riots, the way everything kicked off… they [police] actually are against us that's what a lot of Asians felt like."

Bradford's Muslims are increasingly associated with social alienation and the apparently out-of-control rise in a more universal Islamic extremism. Alam (2006) argues an essentialisation has begun to occur, particularly with Muslims in Bradford; with the events of 7/7 perhaps this now extends to Leeds and other cities.

Stop and search in the context of terrorism has been compared with debates around policing of Black communities in the 1970s and 1980s. Many see the extension of police powers as a return to the infamous 'sus' laws. This inflamed racial tensions and led to the Brixton riots of 1981 in which more than 300 people were injured, including more than 200 police officers. "I felt humiliated. In those days the police thought you were nothing. It didn't matter what you said, their word was worth more than yours. You were made to feel like a thief, even if you hadn't done anything," R Kessie recalls. "This will antagonise young black and Asian kids. It will only make them resent the police more," he says. "They should be trying to engage kids by giving them somewhere to go, like community centres, not hounding them on street corners" (Akwagyiram, 2008). It was interesting to see, given the level of frustration around policing, that very few if any of the young people spoken to felt that bodies such as the Independent Police Complaints Commission (IPCC) were able to help.

The most recent communal disturbances in Britain were seen across the north of England in 2001; the young men in Bradford alluded to the way in which the police behaved both during and post riots and how this affected their relationship with them. That relationship has yet to be fully restored, eight years on. Young people in Burnley have similar sentiments; the trust between them and their local police force seems to have even deteriorated over the last few years. Many feel this is because the police don't understand them and have no desire to understand how young people feel. However, it is fair to say that this is not the scenario everywhere and with every officer, as the example of a Bradford police officer who left a positive impression on one of the participants in the focus group shows:

> *We were waiting for another lad, we were just around the back… just minding our own business and a police woman comes up to us and says 'what are you doing'? So I say to her 'I'm just waiting for my friend'. So she said 'fair enough'; she says 'I'm not gonna search you because you're not up to anything dodgy I can tell, but the people inside don't want you hanging around on the grounds unless you have come here for an actual reason.'*

Muslims in the UK comprise approximately 3% of the whole population; 52% are under the age of 25 – a significant skew towards the younger age groups. However, when we look at prison populations today, we find that Muslims in prison represent 10% of all inmates – more than three times overrepresented, two-thirds of whom are young men aged 18–30 (Prison Service statistics, 2004). Further research is required in this field to better understanding why young Muslims (predominantly men) have found themselves in this position. Some young men in the focus groups spoke of prison life and also commented that in some parts of the country a new inmate need not worry about his safety as he will come across many others from his area, community or town and will have a support network should there be any bullying, etc. This is a reflection of young Muslims themselves finding that some of their peers are either convicted of crimes or have some sort of criminal record.

According to the statistics compiled by the Muslim Youth Helpline, mental health is the second most common issue for their clients (after relationships). Contributory factors to poor mental health include substance, narcotics and alcohol abuse – factors that many young Muslims seem to be increasingly involved in, and which appear to be the primary reasons for imprisonment. Despite religious and cultural taboos, some young Muslims today have a dependency on alcohol (as well as drugs) and regularly binge drink. Due to the religious stigma against the consumption of alcohol and narcotics, young people will find it very challenging to discuss alcohol dependency issues with their parents or other members of the community for fear of being ostracised or labelled.

While many Muslims would like to see a tough stance against alcohol abuse, the fear is that merely penalising young people who are caught with alcohol problematises young people further in a society in which we already have a negative perception of young people. Instead, government strategy needs to consider the reasons why so many young British people turn to drink so frequently and heavily. What are the issues these young people are facing and how do they deal with them? Is drinking alcohol a direct result of other pressures in a young person's life? If so, an investigation into what those issues may be is required in order to remedy the problem in the long term. With debates in 2008 around the extension of the detention period to 42 days and the current context of fears around terrorism, balancing security concerns and civil freedoms has never been more important. Young Muslims feel that their voice is not heard at government level and yet it is *their* personal freedoms that stand to be most at risk.

10
Conclusions

Seen and Not Heard: Voices of Young British Muslims has explored a range of topics that were discussed and debated with youth work students, academics, practitioners and young Muslims themselves from across the UK. The report has brought out the key themes, messages and ideas that have been discussed throughout this research. A range of important issues were raised by the young people that were interviewed individually or in focus groups and are summarised here thematically.

Education

This research has found that education has two key dimensions that have a significant impact on the overwhelming majority of young Muslims:

○   concerns around achievement in light of class structures

○   the impact of parent–school relationships on the young person.

Young Muslims find both areas challenging in different ways and are currently deemed to be disadvantaged on both counts: lack of educational achievement and little or no parental involvement in the school process.

For reasons explained in chapter 5, an active relationship between learning institutions and parents with stable curricula can benefit a young Muslim's experience in education with long-term benefits including positive engagement in society post education. In addition the national curriculum could reflect the interests of ethnic minorities more strongly – for example subjects such as history can often be perceived as 'boring' and/or irrelevant. Should such a subject include post-colonial history in a fair and balanced manner it may be more appealing and relevant to ethnic minorities and aid their knowledge of their heritage. This is done to some extent with Black history, but rarely with the contribution of Arabs or Asians to European civilisation. Young people saw this as an important part of their learning process, "as in knowing what Muslim is and where the background comes from and understanding our own background and where we come from and our parents".

As Khan explores the reconnection with British Muslims, he relates that "it is not just newcomers who should learn the story of who we are as a nation. While every child doing GCSEs knows, quite rightly, all about the story of modern Europe – they know pitiably little about the story of 'us'" (Khan, 2008, p. 14).

History lessons inclusive of the history of Muslims and their interaction with Britain offer the opportunity of empowering young Muslims across schools in the United Kingdom. Such education enables young Muslims to feel they have something to gain by reconnecting and engaging with their histories and their responsibilities. As Khan says: "Making British history compulsory in schools is not just merely about an academic subject, it is about our children understanding who they are" (Khan, 2008, p. 15).

Similarly, an oral history archive would serve to record the valuable stories of early migrants, drawing out and mapping the contribution made by Muslims particularly since the 1940s. This would also enable younger generations to learn more about the older generations and would serve to empower young people as well as enabling them to feel more strongly that they have a stake in 21st-century Britain.

Identity, belonging and citizenship

Questions around loyalty often involve debates on the identity, sense of belonging and citizenship of young British Muslims. Debates on such concepts often neglect the complexities young British Muslims have in terms of their feeling British and others perceiving them as foreigners. Many young Muslims argue their loyalty and belonging lie in the United Kingdom, and along with this comes a sense of citizenship, which allows them to honour their rights and responsibilities as British subjects. Often they are faced with questions that imply that a choice between their religion and nationality needs to be made as the popular perception seems to be that the two are juxtaposed against one another. Young British Muslims comment that for them the two do not contradict one another.

However, on a cultural level Muslims of the second generation sometimes felt pulled between two cultures, and some decided that they would adopt a British Muslim culture while rejecting that of their parents. Among the younger generation, some young Muslims may now be more comfortable in negotiating new identities and the heritage of their parents and grandparents, and we may thus see a partial return to some aspects of traditional culture, for example arranged marriages, in the UK or abroad, with parental involvement, mutual consent and a genuine desire to find marriage partners through the networks and extended families of parents and/or elders and friends.

Community leadership

We have discussed the impact of positive role models and the potential long-term psychological benefits such people may bring to the lives of young British Muslims. This is increasingly apparent due to the currently marked absence of effective leadership and role models within the Muslim communities. Effective leadership and role models can prove to be not only guides and points of advice, often counteracting extremist arguments and thinking, but also serve to create aspirations in young British Muslims. Role models who are successful in their own lives and gain the trust of young British Muslims can enable this young community to understand that they too can achieve their goals; they too can have aspirations.

The gaps between young British Muslims and their parents and grandparents can serve to encourage isolation and non-communication between the generations, especially on matters relating to relationships, sexuality, recreation, etc. as these could be considered culturally and religiously unacceptable. Parents remain ill-equipped to deal with many of these challenges and ironically young people are facing them increasingly in their lives. Factors which contribute to such tensions include language barriers and cultural difference, for example a varied understanding of what constitutes a 'respectful' conversation with one another. Many young British Muslims are unable to find outlets for such issues and frequently discuss them with peers who are also lacking in experience in dealing with such matters. The intergenerational gaps are now (or soon will be) between generations that can speak the same language proficiently and this poses a good opportunity to enhance the value of the conversation. Muslim communities must realise the increasing importance of being able to discuss challenging and controversial issues within the home and should therefore raise better awareness within their communities.

Culturally appropriate and religiously sensitive support and advice services that attract young British Muslims are few in number; we have seen how effective those that do exist can be. An increase in such service provision is necessary to support young people through challenging times.

Media

Young Muslims spoken to during this research seem to have a very negative impression of the media. In essence many of them believe the media will not change its stance on the way it depicts Islam and Muslims and will focus its energies on financial rewards rather than doing right by its audience. Naturally this perception needs to be addressed. However, many others feel a sense of empowerment and motivation in tackling some of the misconceptions around young British Muslims and are taking steps to demystify the stereotypes.

There have been a number of positive stories written about Muslims and/or Islam. In particular, BBC series such as *Islam and Science*, Channel 4's documentaries with Jon Snow and other programmes have offered well-researched and insightful journalism. It is important to distinguish between broadsheets and tabloids and the nature of their material; as well as this we must also acknowledge and give credit to the emergence of more thoughtful, considered pieces of journalism that have helped to move the debate forward within Muslim communities if not always beyond. It is also important to consider the impact of magazines such as *emel*, channels such as al-Jazeera English, the Islam Channel, online presence such as Muslimcafe.tv, the blogosphere and the burgeoning field of 'Muslim journalism'. Due to their recent arrival, such media have not been fully studied, but they deserve some attention. On a day-to-day level the appearance of more Muslim characters (especially young characters) on soaps such as *EastEnders* could be important breakers of cultural barriers and normalisation of Muslims.

Policing and crime

Policing often has many challenges and constraints on its resources; when social structures and places to go are disappearing quickly it is the police who encounter young people on the streets, often in inner-city communities. Policy which seeks to tackle issues young Muslims face requires a more nuanced understanding and perspective on how young Muslims negotiate the pressures of society, family, culture and religion in a world which either essentialises them or ignores their needs. This is particularly important for the police authorities given that some of these young people are turning to substance abuse and the high proportion of young Muslims in prison (indications suggest the two are related). It is not simply a matter of legislation but also an area which requires long-term thinking and understanding the root of the challenges which both the police and young people are tackling. Schemes such as police youth outreach work can often be the first step towards harmonising a police–youth relationship, and demystifying the stereotypes around young Muslims as well as the reputation of certain police authorities.

As found throughout the report, much more investment, of all types and from all the key sectors mentioned, is needed to help Young Muslims to overcome some of the serious challenges that confront them. Kaur-Stubbs recently discussed the investment needed by the government in grassroots communities. In her paper entitled 'Poverty and solidarity' she argues: "A focus on economics over culture, on class over race, is the key to Britain's solidarity and social harmony" (Kaur-Stubbs, 2008). Her argument is that British society is in need of socio-economic support and not just increasing debates on Britishness and the Union Jack. Working-class communities and certainly the many British ethnic minority communities have a lot to offer which can make this country stronger and resilient. It can be argued this strength and resilience lies in the hands of young people; an investment into their futures stands to serve both citizens and country well.

11
Recommendations

A strategic and progressive increase in targeted youth work – faith-based and otherwise – can help guide British Muslims and provide space to explore issues they are tackling around leadership, role models, education and intergenerational experiences. Throughout this research, agencies such as the media, educational institutions and public services have constantly been referred to in conversations and debates with British Muslims. Participants in focus groups, as well as specialists in youth work, have argued that a better informed and responsible approach to Islam and Muslims by such agencies would serve to counteract many of the negative stereotypes and myths surrounding them which will contribute to a relief of the pressure they feel to explain themselves, as well as the way in which they are treated by their non-Muslim counterparts across the UK.

With all the talk of religion and its impact on young people in this report, it is important to point out the risk of artificially reifying religious identity. Though religion will have an overarching impact, the issues need to be dealt with in their own context, i.e. theological issues through a religious prism, youth issues through youth provision, and disengagement issues through social, economic and political structures. In other words not every issue needs to be dealt with through the lens of religion, and in the same way public services do not deal with the faith of Islam but they do work with Muslims – people who happen to believe in Islam.

Government, statutory services and Muslim communities need to reflect on the way they speak about young British Muslims. Instead of perceiving them as the 'problem' they can provide space for discussion and the room for a 'natural' growth for young Muslims as well as faith and culturally sensitive support services, which can assist them in understanding the challenges they face as well as how they can be overcome collectively. Young Muslims seem to face a double whammy of problematisation – the problematisation of Islam and British Muslims, and the problematisation of being young. This often further alienates young Muslims, creating a sense of distrust and leading to disengagement from the very support and guidance services that seek to engage them.

The recommendations presented below have been derived directly from conversations with young people and experts during the course of the research. Implementation of these and further research would serve to address some of the key challenges which young Muslims are grappling with daily.

Investing in the future

1. A national Muslim heritage programme to be funded which looks at capturing the experiences of Muslim pioneers arriving post World War II and integrating into British life. The project would highlight lessons learnt from such experiences which can inform a sense of 'Britishness' for younger Muslims, as well as instilling a sense of local pride and identity, and inspiring greater stakeholdership.

2. Government funding to allow groups providing faith and culturally sensitive counselling and support to extend such work outside London. Every major city in the UK should have support services such as those provided by the Muslim Youth Helpline.

3. Government funding to support youth activities through new small grants programmes over multiple years to achieve longevity.

4. Increased investment by trusts, foundations and bodies such as the National Council for Voluntary Youth Services (NCVYS) into work among young Muslims. This will help organisations to become less reliant on government grants and allows for a greater development of civil society.

Local service providers

1. Joined-up services at the local level (similar to the Integrated Youth Services Hub in Leicester) among agencies whose work impacts on young Muslims and the inclusion of youth and community representatives on these teams.

2. Local service providers need to find ways to work directly with a wider range of young people, for example the 'Youth Offer', which aims to reflect the needs of all young people through their participation at a local level.

3. Regeneration projects in areas with strong concentrations of Muslims should take particular account of the needs that may be specific to young Muslims, especially at the planning phase of service delivery. Enhancements in consultation, information provision and assessment processes will enable service providers to identify how services can better match their service provision to meet the needs of young Muslims which may be currently overlooked.

4. Targeted and high-quality support for professionals working with young Muslims to understand specific religious and cultural challenges facing them and the barriers to accessing state youth services.

5. More focused, assertive mentoring and work-based learning schemes offering development plans. These should use quick and direct feedback mechanisms and present the opportunity to increase skills as well as offer information, advice, guidance and possible routes to employment and/or educational opportunities.

Education and schools

1. Use the new duty on schools to promote community cohesion to enable better integration of Muslims into British society through:

    a. Muslim heritage and contribution to civilisation past and present encompassed into aspects of teaching, learning and curricula.

    b. Direct academic intervention programmes being focused on Muslim boys to achieve the equity and excellence strand of the new duty.

    c. Schools becoming 'safe and neutral places' for local communities to come together and interact with one another. School outreach programmes could look at how to directly meet the learning needs of Muslim parents and wider communities that are currently inhibited from full participation in civil and political life.

2. Long-term school-linking exchange programmes between schools with young people from different ethnic profiles embedded within school ethos with the purpose of ensuring that more meaningful relationships are formed.

3. Schools should create opportunities for elderly Muslims to speak to younger Muslims. Examples of work amongst Gypsy and Traveller communities as well as white working-class groups in some London boroughs shows that such intergenerational encounters work well. Often the best projects are two-way processes where young people teach older generations new skills and older people teach young people life skills.

Muslim voluntary sector and mosques

1. Mosques should have dedicated outreach programmes services and facilities to meet the needs of young people.

2. Management committees in Mosques should ensure that Imams and community leaders who engage with youth have adequate training in meeting the needs of young people.

3. Voluntary sector organisations can reach a sizeable number of young Muslims; such organisations would benefit from specialised youth skills training.

4. Through mentoring and educational support programmes (such as projects initiated by Mosaic and the City Circle), Muslim professionals could significantly invest in the development of young people.

5. Increasingly madrasahs are teaching more than rote learning. This needs more concerted attention and madrasahs need to teach the understanding of the text as well as relating it to the lived reality of young British Muslims.

Media

1. There is a need for more events such as workshops that can enhance media literacy among young people and give increased contact with journalists and

programme makers, as well as provide an opportunity to air concerns and anxieties, to create two-way conversations.

2. Employers in the media should increase awareness of recruitment opportunities and career pathways in the industry, specifically targeting young Muslims.

Policing

1. The police should create more avenues for young people to better understand police services, shadow officers and interact in ways that can develop learning in both directions.

2. The police should work with non-police partners to inform young people of their rights and responsibilities as well as complaints procedures regarding policing. This is particularly important when young Muslims are feeling targeted by measures such as 'stop and search'.

3. The Independent Police Complaints Commission (IPCC) should develop partnerships with suitable Muslim organisations to collate data on complaints about police procedures from Muslim citizens (given that some young Muslims may be reluctant to approach the IPCC directly).

Further research

1. Increased funding for targeted, thematic research into the specific areas highlighted in this report.

2. A revisit of the Cantle Report (2001) and an assessment of the progress on matters relating to cohesion and young people, eight years on, especially in light of the 2007 duty on schools to promote cohesion.

3. There is a need to examine the use of terminology such as cohesion, Preventing Violent Extremism (PVE) and integration. For many these terms have become synonymous with the use of social vehicles to achieve political outcomes. As a result many local communities resist (even resent) the terms and therefore may not engage in the discourse.

12
Bibliography

Abbas, T. (2004) *The Education of British South Asians: Ethnicity, capital and class structure.* Basingstoke: Palgrave Macmillan.

Akwagyiram, A. (2008) 'Is stop and search a good idea?' See http://news.bbc.co.uk/1/hi/uk/7218680.stm (accessed 28 May 2008).

Alam, M. Y. (2006) *Made in Bradford.* Pontefract: Route Publishing.

Association of Muslim Schools (2007) Q & A Muslim Schools. See http://news.bbc.co.uk/1/hi/education/6338219.stm (accessed 20 April 2009).

Brake, M. (1990) *Comparative Youth Culture: The sociology of youth cultures and youth subcultures in America, Britain and Canada.* London: Routledge.

Cantle, T. (Chair) (2001) *Community Cohesion Report: A report of the Independent Review Team.* London: Home Office.

Cassen, R. and Kingdon, G. (2007) *Tackling Low Educational Achievement.* York: Joseph Rowntree Foundation.

The Children's Society (2008) 'UK failing to meet children's mental health and well-being needs', 24 April. See www.childrenssociety.org.uk/

whats_happening/media_office/latest_news/7092_pr.html (accessed November 2008).

The Children's Society (2009) 'Thinking about my life'. See http://sites.childrenssociety.org.uk/mylife/home.aspx (accessed 15 January 2009).

Coleman, J. S. (1961) *The Adolescent Society*. New York: Free Press.

Coles, M. I. (2005) *Faithful and Proud. Young British Muslim Conference Report*. Leicester: School Development Support Agency.

DCLG (2008) *The Next Generation of Muslim Community Leaders*. London: Department of Communities and Local Government. See www.communities.gov.uk/news/corporate/987399 (accessed 15 January 2009).

DCSF (2007) *National Curriculum Assessment, GCSE and Equivalent Attainment and Post-16 Attainment by Pupil Characteristics, in England 2006/07*. London: Department for Children, Schools and Families.

Department of Sociology (University of Bristol) (2003) 'Sociological approaches to youth'. See www.bristol.ac.uk/sociology/prospective/undergraduates/third/youth.html (accessed 5 June 2008).

Downes, D. (1966) *The Delinquent Solution*. London: Routledge & Kegan Paul.

Department for Work and Pensions (2006) *A New Deal for Welfare: Empowering people to work*. London: The Stationery Office.

Green, H. et al. (2004) *Mental Health of Children and Young People in Great Britain*. London: Office of National Statistics.

Home Office (2004) 'Statistics on race and the criminal justice system'. See www.homeoffice.gov.uk/rds/ (accessed 16 June 2008).

Husain, M. G. (2004) *Muslim Youth and Madrasa Education*. New Delhi: Institute of Objective Studies.

Jacobson, J. (1998) *Islam in Transition: Religion and identity among British Pakistani youth.* Oxon: Routledge.

Jawad, H. (2008) *Forgotten Voices: Developing more effective engagement with Muslim youth and communities.* London: Forward Thinking.

Kaur-Stubbs, R. (2008) Chapter 3: 'Poverty and solidarity', in Johnson, N. (ed.) *Citizenship, Cohesion and Solidarity.* London: The Smith Institute.

Kelly, R. (2005) 'Foreword' in Depatment for Education and Skills *Youth Matters.* London: Stationery Office.

Khan, S. (2008) *Fairness not Favours: How to reconnect with British Muslims.* London: Fabian Society.

Layard, R. et al. (2009) *A Good Childhood: Searching for values in a competitive age.* London: Penguin.

Leicestershire Constabulary. See www.leics.police.uk/files/library/documents/street_interventions.pdf (accessed 5 March 2009).

Lewis, P. (1994) *Islamic Britain: Religion, politics and identity among British Muslims: Bradford in the 1990s.* London: I. B. Tauris.

Lewis, P. (2007) *Young, British and Muslim.* London: Continuum International Publishing.

Malik, A. (2006) *The State We Are In: Identity, Terror and the Law of Jihad.* Bristol: Amal Press.

Malik, R. et al. (2007) *Providing Faith and Culturally Sensitive Support Services to Young British Muslims.* Leicester: National Youth Agency.

Ministry of Education (1960) *The Youth Service in England and Wales* ('The Albemarle Report'), London: HMSO.

Model Learning. See www.modellearning.com (accessed 9 January 2009).

Murdock, G. and McCron, R. (1973) 'Scoobies, skin and contemporary pop', *New Society*, vol. 23, no. 247.

Murdock, G. and McCron, R. (1976) 'Consciousness of class and consciousness of generation', in Hall, S. and Jefferson, T. (eds) *Resistance Through Rituals*. London: Hutchinson.

Murtuja, B. (2006) *Muslim Youth Speak*. Leeds: Hamara Centre.

Muslim Council of Britain (2005) *Muslim Voices*, interim report. London: Muslim Council of Britain.

Muslim Youth Helpline, 'Issues'. See www.myh.org.uk/information.php?id=2 (accessed October 2008).

National Youth Agency (2009) *England's Local Authority Youth Services: The NYA audit 2007-08*. Leicester: National Youth Agency.

ONS (2001) *Census 2001*. Office for National Statistics. See www.statistics.gov.uk (accessed 14 July 2008).

Ouseley, H. (2001) *The Bradford District Race Review*. Bradford: Bradford Vision.

Patel, H. (2007) Radio programme on *Gangsters*. Leicester: BBC Radio Leicester. See www.bbc.co.uk/leicester/local_radio/ (accessed December 2007).

Prison Service statistics (2004) Cited on National Youth Agency website, available at www.nya.org.uk/information/108761/ukmuslimcommunitystatistics/ (accessed October 2008).

Saeed, A. et al. (1999) 'New ethnic and national questions in Scotland: post-British identities among Glasgow Pakistani teenagers', *Ethnic and Racial Studies*, vol. 22, no. 5.

Saltley Inquiry. See https://www.tes.co.uk/article.aspx?storycode=376375 (accessed 10 March 2009).

The Scout Association. See https://members.scouts.org.uk/cms.php?pageid=6 (accessed 10 March 2009).

Seddon, M. et al. (2003) *British Muslims: Loyalty and Belonging*. Leicester: The Islamic Foundation.

Sen, A. (2006) *Identity and Violence: The illusion of destiny*. London: Penguin.

Sugarman, B. (1967) 'Involvement in youth culture, academic achievement and conformity in school', *British Journal of Sociology*, June, pp. 151–64.

Wilson, J. (2008) 'Stop and search'. See www.stopandsearch.com/why%2Dits%2Ddone/ (accessed 20 May 2008).

Young Citizens (2003) *Saltley Inquiry*. Birmingham: Young Citizens.

Young People for Life project. See www.yp4l.com/ (accessed 10 March 2009).

Youth at the United Nations (2003) 'Youth in extreme poverty: dimensions and country responses', Chapter 3 in Curtain, R. (2003) *World Youth Report 2003: the global situation of young people*. New York: United Nations.